TEN MILLION BAYONETS

Below: A platoon of T-54s advancing at high speed, yielding extremely visible dust clouds. Soviet tanks can supplement this by injecting raw diesel fuel into their hot exhausts, creating dense smoke screens. (*Armor* magazine)

TEN

MILLION BAYONETS

Inside the Armies of the Soviet Union

David C. Isby

ARMS AND ARMOUR PRESS
London   New York   Sydney

Below: A Soviet ski team is inserted by Mi-8 Hips. Special forces, like paratroopers, are good candidates for specialized ski missions, being tough, fit, and having complete pre-conscription training that allows conscripts time to absorb new specialities.

First published in Great Britain in 1988 by Arms and Armour Press, Artillery House, Artillery Row, London SW1P 1RT.

Distributed in the USA by Sterling Publishing Co. Inc., 2 Park Avenue, New York, NY 10016.

Distributed in Australia by Capricorn Link (Australia) Pty. Ltd., P.O. Box 665, Lane Cove, New South Wales 2066, Australia.

British Library Cataloguing in Publication Data:
Isby, David C.
Ten million bayonets
1. Union of Soviet Socialist Republics *Armi ia*
2. Arms and armour – Soviet Union
I. Title
623.4'0947   UU820.S/

ISBN 0-85368-774-9

Jacket illustration colour simulation by Robert W. Phasey. Reproduced by Courtesy of Novosti Press Agency.

The illustrations in this book have been collected from many sources, and vary in quality owing to the variety of circumstances under which they were taken and preserved. As a result, certain of the illustrations are not of the standard to be expected from the best of today's equipment, materials and techniques. They are nevertheless included for their inherent information value, to provide an authentic visual coverage of the subject.

Designed and edited by DAG Publications Ltd. Designed by David Gibbons; edited by Michael Boxall; typeset by Typesetters (Birmingham) Ltd., camerawork by M&E Graphics, North Fambridge, Essex; printed and bound in Great Britain by The Bath Press, Avon.

CONTENTS

Below: These are the sort of troopers to be found in the *Spetsnaz*,
here wearing the camouflage suits and striped vest of the paratroopers.
They are tough, fit and airborne-qualified.

INTRODUCTION

RUSSIANS like to think that the torch of Western civilization was passed from Rome to Byzantium to Moscow. In fact, what was passed down was the technique of practising imperial power. The principle of government control by force in the land of Russia, dating back to the time of the Mongols, has come down through Ivan the Terrible and Stalin to Comrade Gorbachev. Much of his domain is not the homeland of the Russian people, but is conquered territory, following imperial expansion at the same time that Britain and France were similarly expanding into Africa. While the British and French conquests are now independent, those of the Russians remain firmly integrated into the Soviet Union.

The division of the Soviet Union into sixteen Military Districts — miniature war economies — dates back to Tsarist times, and recognizes the linked civil and military nature of the state. As, in the final analysis, the power of Rome was in the *gladii* of its legions, and that of Byzantium in the lances of its *cataphracts*, the power of the Soviet Union rests on the ten million bayonets, serving and first-line reserve (counting all reservists gives a total of more than twenty million), of its army.

The Soviets may be cynical in their view of Lenin's ideology, but its impact cannot be ignored. Marxism-Leninism perceives Capitalism as the threat, a perception which is reinforced by Russian nationalism and xenophobia which, in turn, demand the maintenance of a military force that is not only large and absorbing of resources, but involves all aspects of Soviet society.

This book takes a look at different parts of the Soviet Army and the hardware they use: a tank division in the Western USSR with their T-80 tanks, poised to drive deep into western Europe; a motorized rifle brigade in Afghanistan with BMP infantry fighting vehicles, fighting a long and brutal war; an artillery division in East Germany with long-range multiple rocket-launchers, ready to provide the firepower for a war in Europe; an air assault brigade, also in East Germany, with its helicopters; a special operations brigade in the Southern USSR, poised for operations against southern Asia; an airborne division in Siberia, part of the Soviet presence in Asia, and their anti-tank weapons; and a Naval Infantry brigade deployed opposite Scandinavia. These all show different weapons, missions, and aspects of the Soviet military. It is not a complete or comprehensive picture, but it should show how the Soviets intend, if war comes again, to win.

The Soviet Army is a mixture of the superlative and the inadequate, of rigid discipline and a vagabond laxness, all mixed together. There are deep flaws throughout the fabric of the Soviet Army, in the weapons, in the tactics, in the way it uses its men. But there are also a great many strengths. The Army which helped put an end to the Third Reich and entered Berlin has not become a bunch of bungling black marketeers. Much like the wartime British or US Armies, the Soviet Army is big and inefficient, but not ineffective. The Soviet Army does not have to be the best in the world. It does not have to be as good, man for man or division for division, as its opponent. It has to win, for defeat may mean the end of everyone and everything. That is something the Soviets do not intend to permit.

Below: The 41st Guards Tank Division is first and foremost a combined-arms force. The Soviets have stressed mobile air defence as an integral part of combined-arms tactics., This includes the ZSU-23-4, the standard Soviet self-propelled anti-aircraft gun, mounting a quadruple 23mm automatic cannon with an on-vehicle *Gun Dish* radar. It was extensively used in the 1973 Middle East War and accounted for most of the approximately 40 Israeli aircraft lost to ground fire. Now over 20 years old, it is to be replaced by the ZSU-30-2. (US Navy)

1

41ST GUARDS TANK DIVISION, ARTEMOVSK, KIEV MILITARY DISTRICT, USSR

EVEN to jaded modern sensibilities, the sights and sounds of a Soviet division on the march are still an awesome experience. Russia is still a country of unpaved roads, and dust or mud inevitably accompany the clash and grind of the vehicles, as do the curses of the crewmen repairing those that have broken down. No one can truly understand blitz-krieg warfare until he has participated in the repair of a thrown track.

The columns of hundreds of tanks, BMP infantry fighting vehicles and the long lines of supply trucks, all responding to the orders of the divisional commander from the knot of armoured vehicles that make up his forward command post, is indeed, as Sir Colin Campbell said when he saw the Russian cavalry massing to charge the 'Thin Red Line' at Balaclava, 'a sight you'll nae see coming down the Gallogate'.

The 41st Guards Tank Division goes on the march in full strength only about twice a year, as part of the series of grand manoeuvres that ends each 6-month training cycle. But when the division moves, it does so with a mobility far greater than that of the panzers that raced for the Meuse in 1940. One former Soviet soldier, a tank driver in a tank division like the 41st, remembers how, in the 1970s, his regiment covered 320 kilometres on its own tracks in 24 hours. Two tanks failed to complete the march – both drivers were court-martialled – but the other 93 would have been there to fight at the end of the day.

THE TANK AND THE SOVIET ARMY

Combining both fire-power and mobility, the tank is the linchpin of the Soviet Army. Its importance had been realized long before the Germans invaded Russia in

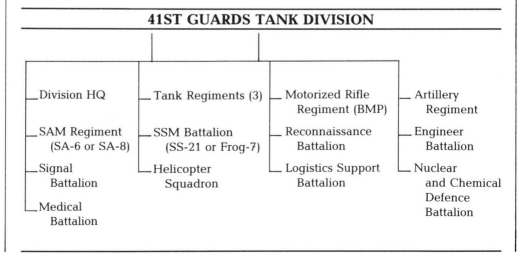

41ST GUARDS TANK DIVISION

- Division HQ
- SAM Regiment (SA-6 or SA-8)
- Signal Battalion
- Medical Battalion
- Tank Regiments (3)
- SSM Battalion (SS-21 or Frog-7)
- Helicopter Squadron
- Motorized Rifle Regiment (BMP)
- Reconnaissance Battalion
- Logistics Support Battalion
- Artillery Regiment
- Engineer Battalion
- Nuclear and Chemical Defence Battalion

Left: The T-34-85 equipped the 41st Guards Tank Division when it was formed from a wartime tank corps. While no longer in first-line Soviet service, they remain in Soviet war reserve stocks and are used in action in the Third World. This Kabul regime T-34-85 was knocked out in the summer of 1979 in the Jadji district of Paktia province, Afghanistan. Standing in front is Sayid Hassan Gailani, one of the leaders of the National Islamic Front of Afghanistan, a Resistance party. (Hassan Gailani)

1941. During the Civil War (1917–22) fire-power and mobility had had to be improvised; the armoured train and far-ranging cavalry forces with their troika-pulled machine-gun carts were the dominant weapons, but the few armoured cars and tanks on each side impressed the men who would create the future Red Army. They realized that the new Soviet Union would need not just a few tanks to support infantry, as the Western Allies had used them in 1917–18, but entire mechanized armies, especially if the Soviet Union were to be surrounded by states hostile to its regime.

In the 1920s, however, the Red Army could afford little in the way of weaponry, but they had plenty of ideas. By the 1930s, they had formulated the tactics of the deep-penetrating mechanized offensive, with far-ranging tank forces replacing the cavalry armies of the Civil War. But the men who conceived these ideas perished in the Great Purge, and the Soviet tank

force, on the eve of the German invasion in 1941, was certainly not capable of using the tactics envisaged in the 1930s.

In 1941, most of the Russian tanks were old and few spare parts were available, but there were a small number of the latest models, and these compared favourably with the tanks of any other nation. Indeed, the T-34 medium tank proved a great surprise to the Germans, who found it superior to any of their individual tanks.

Having lost most of their army in the first year of the war, the Soviets set about creating a new one. With the T-34 coming off production lines in the Urals in quantity, they were able to field powerful tank forces, a high proportion of which were deployed in combined arms tank and mechanized corps. These were the most important Soviet forces in the battles of 1942–45; the masses of Soviet rifle divisions, with their horse-drawn transport, lacking the crucial mix of fire-power and mobility that combat in Russia required.

TO THE RHINE: THE SOVIET FRONT OFFENSIVE

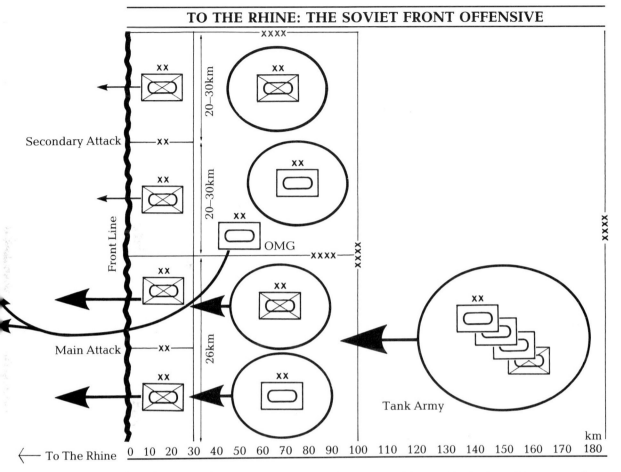

Decisive penetration, or the counter-attacking of enemy penetration called for mechanized, combined arms forces fielding reliable tanks that could sustain intense combat. Today, the 41st Guards Tank Division is an heir of the army that won the War in the East in 1945, its 'Guards' title being a battle honour commemorating a wartime exploit.

THE TANK DIVISION AND THE SOVIET ARMY

The mission of all of the Soviet's 62 tank divisions is to gain victory on the battlefield whether in western Europe, Manchuria, or southern Asia, with or without the use of nuclear weapons. Tank and motorized rifle divisions, grouped into armies (of three to four divisions) and fronts (of about four armies), are the basic tactical units.

The main role of the 41st, like other Soviet tank divisions, is that of exploita-

tion. Motorized rifle formations or nuclear or chemical strikes will make a gap through which the tank divisions can move to clinch the victory, as did the British armour at El Alamein. But the Soviets hope that if they can surprise or paralyze the enemy there will be no defensive line to breach, and the tank divisions will use their capability for movement and firepower in a series of meeting engagements.

Tank divisions such as the 41st can be used as Operational Manoeuvre Groups (OMGs), successors to the wartime Mobile Groups which penetrated gaps in the extended German defences that were overstretched by Hitler's 'stand-fast' orders. Deployed behind the first echelon of Soviet forces, they will advance through an exploitable gap – caused by surprise, speed or firepower – to move on an objective in what the Soviets call the 'operational rear' of an enemy, up to 250 kilometres away; objectives that can include bridges, headquarters, key terrain features, or a capital city. The OMG contributes to the Soviet capacity to 'fight deep' in the enemy rear.

The Soviets, today, would rather have surprise than numerical superiority, especially if it came to a war in Europe. If they could cross the Inner German Border before NATO's forces were in their General Defensive Positions (in place for the forward defence), the tank divisions would be in their element. Surprise, shock, speed and manoeuvre would form the basic battle plan of the 41st's commander.

The 41st Guards Tank Division's garrison location at Kiev Military District, in the Ukraine, puts it not only in excellent tank country for training, but in what the Soviets call the Second Operational Echelon. In any future offensive the troops from the military districts in European Russia would form the follow-on to the forces in East Germany, Poland, and Czechoslovakia.

If the Soviets are to have numerical superiority on a battlefield in Europe, they will need those divisions that are stationed in the Soviet Union itself. The forces in eastern Europe cannot overwhelm NATO by weight of numbers. NATO's 'Follow On Forces Attack' (FOFA) is basically to strengthen the conventional forces in western Europe so that they can stop Soviet and Warsaw Pact thrusts from East Germany and Czechoslovakia while deep-strike forces – such as Tornado strike aircraft – block the arrival of forces from European Russia. Just as the 41st's opponents would be ineffective if surprised, the 41st would be equally ineffective if kept off the battlefield by such means as destroying the bridges over the Oder or the Vistula or blocking the roads into Germany.

THE TANKS OF THE 41ST

All tactics and all other equipment in the Soviet Army exist basically to get the tanks where the men in the Kremlin want them to go. If ever the Soviets feel the tank is obsolete, they will need a whole new army, because the one they have would then no longer work.

Soviet tank design is evolutionary in most respects – a new vehicle about every ten years and substantial improvements in existing ones every five years. This process started with the wartime T-34/85 tank, considered by many to be the finest tank of the war. In 1944, the T-34/85 was stretched to replace the 85mm gun with a 100mm gun, creating the 1944-model T-44, which, in turn, begat the T-54–T-55 series, many thousands of which were produced from 1947 to 1979. These tanks have been involved in just about every conflict world-wide since the 1950s. During the production run, they introduced many improvements – including nuclear, biological and chemical protective systems and laser rangefinders, among others – but kept the same engine and the 100mm gun. By replacing the T-55's 100mm rifled gun with a 115mm smoothbore, the Soviets devel-

Below: T-55 tanks bringing fraternal socialist greetings to the people of Prague in 1968. The 41st took part in this operation, and the projection of political power over the nations of the Warsaw Pact remains one of its missions, in common with those of all Soviet forces in the western Soviet Union, as was seen in the 1981 mobilization against Poland. (US Information Agency)

oped the T-62, which entered service in 1961 and, although out of production today, is still a first-line Soviet main battle tank. The T-62 is also a veteran of many conflicts; in particular the 1973 Middle East War. All of these tanks use the same basic lightweight engine from the 1930s, and the same type of suspension.

The 41st used each type of new tank as it came into service. The tank divisions in European Russia are normally the first to receive new equipment, even before those in East Germany and certainly before those in Central Asia or on the Chinese border. The 41st, however, received one honour that, in retrospect, it might rather have missed. It was selected to be the first division to receive a revolutionary new

main battle tank, the T-64, when it went into service in 1967. The T-64 broke from the standard Soviet evolutionary approach, introducing not only a new gun – a 125mm smoothbore – but a new engine and suspension and a stereo-coincidence range-finder where earlier tanks had all used a simple stadiametric rangefinder.

Unfortunately for the Soviets, this great leap forward in tank design had one fault. It did not work. Non-working tanks are fine in some Third-World countries, where they are used only for parades and coups, but for the Soviet Army, it was, to say the least, a major drawback. The result was that the T-64 had extensive developmental and production problems, despite its advances. For years, the 41st bore the

Right: A T-62 tank, captured from Arab forces in the 1973 War, is examined by GIs. The 1973 War provided the West with a technical intelligence windfall on 1960s-vintage Soviet hardware that has not been repeated since. (US Army)

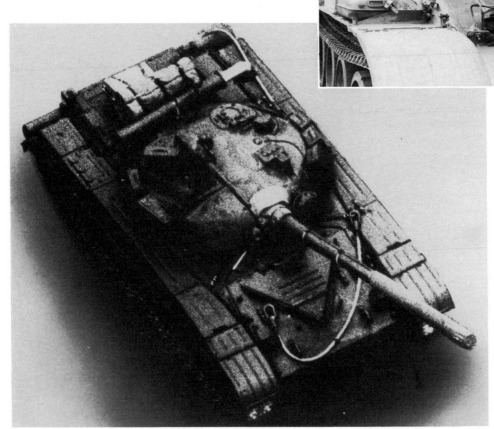

Left: The T-64 main battle tank. The 41st Guards had the dubious honour of being the first division to be equipped with this tank during its long and difficult development. (US Department of Defense)

Below: The T-72 main battle tank. Cheaper than the T-64, it is more reliable and has been widely exported. It is replacing T-55s in much of the Soviet Army. (US Department of Defense)

Right: It is probably the T-80 main battle tank that currently equips the 41st Guards Tank Division. It combines high-technology systems and high performance while apparently avoiding the reliability problems of the T-64. (US Department of Defense)

brunt of them. Viktor Suvorov, a former Soviet officer who served in the 41st, reports that T-64s were nicknamed 'the steel graves' and factory technicians had to be kept permanently on hand to keep the tanks running.

The problems were eventually resolved, after a fashion. Today, T-64s are front-line equipment in Group Soviet Forces Germany and some divisions in the western Military Districts of the Soviet Union. Yet this complex tank was never exported and it is unlikely that it will go into wider service. According to the US Department of Defense, T-64 production ceased in 1982, although some analysts think this happened in the 1970s.

The T-64B version, apparently only produced in limited numbers, is armed with AT-8 Kobra anti-tank guided missiles (NATO codename: Songster), a little-known weapon that is fired out of a gun tube like the US Shillelagh used by the M60A2 main battle tank or the experimental French ACRA system. This use of guided missiles, fired from the tank's 125mm gun tube, provides better long-range fire power than the normal 125mm smoothbore, which, while having a high muzzle velocity and good penetration, lacks accuracy above 1,500–2,000 metres' range.

In the late 1960s, the Soviets decided to redesign the T-64 in a bid to change its innovative but mechanically troublesome suspension and engine. The result was the T-72, which used the same basic suspension and engine as all the preceding main battle tanks. It retained the advanced fire control systems and improved nuclear, biological and chemical warfare protection

of the T-64. The 125mm gun is reportedly fully stabilized, allowing a shoot-on-the-move capability. The T-72 has apparently done a lot better than the T-64 and is in large-scale production and has been widely exported. Soviet T-72s have been in action in Afghanistan; Iraqi and Syrian T-72s have also seen much combat.

Late model T-72s differ from early versions in details – improved armour on the turret, smoke or decoy launchers on the turret sides, different arrangement of the optics for the laser rangefinder (which early production T-72s did not have). They also have replaced the folding 'gill' armour plates which protected the tank's flank on the T-64 and earlier T-72 models by a detachable skirt of Kevlar-like fabric

41ST GUARDS TANK DIVISION

MEN	11,750
T-64 and T-80 Tanks	326
BMP-1 and BMP-2 IFV	228
BRM and BRM-1 recon vehicle	19
BRDM-2 scout car	29
152mm SP howitzer M-1973 2S3	48
122mm SP howitzer M-1974 2S1	96
BM-21 122mm MRL	24
SS-21 surface-to-surface missile	4
SA-6 SP SAM launcher	20
SA-13 SP SAM launcher	16
ZSU-23-4 SP AA gun	16
BRDM-2 SP ATGM launcher	9
Mi-2 Hoplite light helicopter	6
Mi-8 Hip medium helicopter	8
Mi-24 Hind-E attack helicopter	6
SA-7 or SA-14 SAM launcher	93
RPG-16 AT weapon	469
RPK-74 5.45mm LMG	526

armour over the suspension and external fuel tanks. This arrangement is apparently intended to give protection against the 20mm and 25mm Bushmaster cannon carried on infantry fighting vehicles such as the German Marder and the US M2 Bradley.

The T-64 and T-72 disturbed NATO. They had counted on the superiority of individual NATO tanks to counter the Soviet's traditional numerical superiority.

By the mid-1970s, Soviet design improvements in existing types of tanks, together with the introduction of new tanks, not to mention new tactical and operational concepts to use them more effectively, began to show the West that the Soviets could have quantity without forsaking quality.

Following the T-72 came the T-80, which probably now equips much, if not all, of the 41st. Basically, it is a more reliable follow-on to the T-64, using the same weapons,

TANKS

	T-54/55	T-62	T-64	T-72	T-80
Crew	4 (cmdr, driver, gunner, loader)	4 (cmdr, driver, gunner, loader)	3 (cmdr, driver, gunner)	3 (cmdr, driver, gunner)	3 (cmdr, driver, gunner)
Weight (mt)	36.0	37.5	38.0	41.0	42.0
Length (gun forward) (m)	9.00	9.33	9.10	9.20	9.20
Width overall (m)	3.14	3.30	3.40	3.60	3.60
Height overall (m)	2.20	2.40	2.30	2.30	2.30
Engine	V-12 520hp (T-54) (T-54) 580hp (T-55) diesel	V-12 580hp diesel	5-cyl 700–750hp diesel multifuel	V-12 780hp diesel	V-12 1200hp gas turbine
Max. road speed (km/hr)	50	50	50	50	60
Fuel capacity (litres)	800 (T-54) 960 (T-55)	960	1,000	1,000	1,000
Road range (km)	400 (T-54) 500 (T-55) (715w/aux fueltanks)	450 (650w/aux fueltanks)	450 (600w/aux fueltanks)	450 (600w/aux fueltanks)	350 (500w/aux fueltanks)
Trench crossing (m)	2.70	2.80	2.70	2.70	2.70
Vertical step (m)	0.80	0.80	0.80	0.80	0.80
Max. gradient	30°	30°	30°	30°	30°
Fording (m)	1.4/5.5 w/snorkel	1.4/5.5 w/snorkel	1.4/5.5 w/snorkel	1.4/5.5 w/snorkel	1.4/5.5 w/snorkel
Armour:[1]					
Hull (mm)	99	102	400	400	500
Turret (mm)	203	242	400	400	500
NBC Protection	PAZ radiation detection system	PAZ radiation detection system	filtration & over-pressure system & PAZ radiation detection system	filtration & over-pressure system & PAZ radiation detection system	filtration & over-pressure system & PAZ radiation detection system

including a 'B' model with the Kobra ATGM used in the T-64B. Engine, suspension, and automatic gun loader, three of the T-64's weak spots, are reported to have been improved, as have the types of armour.

The Soviets have been working for years on their own version of high-technology advances over standard rolled homogeneous steel armour plate. The new armour is probably fitted to the T-64, T-72 and the T-80. Less advanced than the British-designed Chobham armour used in the West, the Soviets' 'combined armour' on this tank appears to be steel backed by a layer of ceramic to act as a backstop against the force of a shaped-charge explosion.

In addition, Soviet tanks are now using active armour, similar to the Israeli 'Blazer' system. These shirt-box like additions to tank armour, seen widely in news photo-

TANKS

	T-54/55	T-62	T-64	T-72	T-80
Introduced	1949 (T-54) 1958 (T-55)	1961	late 1960s	early 1970s	early 1980s
Gun calibre (mm)	100	115	125 AT-8 ATGM	125	125 AT-8 ATGM
Type	rifled tank gun	smoothbore tank gun	smoothbore tank gun or missile-launcher	smoothbore tank gun	smoothbore tank gun or missile-launcher
Elevation (degrees)	$-4°-+17°$ (T-54) $-5°-+18°$ (T-55)	$-5°-+18°$	$-5°-+18°$	$-5°-+18°$	$-5°-+18°$
Rate of fire (rpm)	5–7	3–5	6–8	6–8	6–8
Ammunition (types)	Frag-HE HEAT HVAP-T AP-T, APDS, APC-T	Frag-HE (FS), HEAT-FS, HVAP-FSDS	Frag-HE (FS), HEAT-FS HVAP-FSDS	Frag-HE (FS), HEAT-FS HVAP-FSDS	Frag-HE (FS), HEAT-FS HVAP-FSDS
Maximum Range (m)	21,000	20,000	20,000+	20,000+	20,000+
Effective Range 50% Ph (m)	1,500	1,600	2,000	2,000	2,000
Armour Penetration (mm @ ° obliquity @ 1,000m)	200 HVAP-T 180 AP-T & APC-T 390 HEAT any range	230 HVAP-FSDS 450 HEAT-FS any range	300+ HVAP-FASDS 475+ HEAT-FS any range	300+ HVAP-FSDS 475+ HEAT-FS any range	300+ HVAP-FSDS 475+ HEAT-FS any range
Basic load (rd)	34 (T-54) 43 (T-55)	40	40	40	40
Secondary armament	1×12.7mm 2×7.62mm (T-55)	1×12.7mm 1×7.62mm	1×12.7mm 1×7.62mm	1×12.7mm 1×7.62mm	1×12.7mm 1×7.62mm

[1]Equivalent/maximum.

Left: A T-80 shows the characteristic exhaust – differing from the usual pipes – that suggests it is the first Soviet main battle tank to be powered by a turbine engine. (US Department of Defense)

graphs from the 1982 Lebanon War, contain a fast-acting explosive. When hit by a shaped-charge projectile, they themselves explode, the intention being to blow out the explosive cone of the warhead like an oil well fire being dynamited. The Soviet version uses smaller explosive boxes than the Israeli version.

Although the T-80 lacks the 'boxy' sides of Chobham-type compound armour, it features, as well as a laser rangefinder, active armour protection over the top decking to protect it against shaped-charge attack from above, such as from anti-tank bomblets; and a pair of devices which look like smoke mortars, but may also be used to fire chaff and flares to decoy various precision-guided munitions that would rely either on radar or infra-red inputs for weapons guidance. The T-80 is coming off Soviet production lines at a considerable rate – 1,200 in 1982, as opposed to 1,300 earlier T-72 versions.

The T-80 is currently the most advanced main battle tank in production, but the Soviets are working on an even more advanced tank. Since the 1930s, Soviets tanks have always been among the best in the world and it is unlikely that they are going to fall behind.

Tanks such as the T-72 and the T-80 are less vulnerable than preceding Soviet tanks. By the early 1980s, anti-tank guided missiles such as the US TOW and Dragon and the European MILAN were unable to penetrate the frontal armour of these

tanks, which lead to the design of a whole range of new weapons and warheads. But neither the T-72 nor the T-80 is invulnerable. The Israelis destroyed a number of Syrian T-72s in Lebanon in 1982, apparently by tanks firing advanced 105mm ammunition, or TOW anti-tank guided missiles, fitted with an improved Israeli-made warhead, fired from AH-1 attack helicopters.

Like all Soviet tanks, the T-72 and the T-80 are offensive weapons, and are not intended to take punishment. Major-General Moshe Bar Kochba, commander of the Israeli Armoured Corps said: 'The T-72 is equipped with ultra-modern optical systems. Its strong fire-power, penetrative, zeroing-in and destructive capabilities are its most impressive feature.' It is not known whether the Syrian 'export' versions of the T-72s had combined armour; the Soviets seldom put their most sensitive subsystems on export tanks.

The T-64, T-72 and T-80 all use the Soviet 125mm smoothbore gun with an automatic loading system, which means that they have 3-man crews, as opposed to standard 4-man crews. The 41st had the privilege of being the first to discover, when first issued with T-64s, that the only drawback was that this wonder of Soviet technology did more damage to its users than to its targets. The gun automatically elevates to load – necessitated by the small size of the turret. The autoloader's grippers align a shell and charge with the breech from the two-level carousel-type holder at the turret rear. A power rammer then rams them into the automatically operating horizontal sliding breech. Apparently this loading system has a tendency to grab the gunner and attempt to load *him* into the breech. In the words of one US Army officer 'We believe that this is how the Red Army Chorus gets its soprano section.' The Russians solved this problem eventually, but it shows that improving weapons technology is seldom easy.

Even the 41st's T-80s are not better than the US M1 Abrams or the British Challenger. The T-80 is, because of its evolutionary design, less advanced. Soviet 'combined armour' is probably not as good as the NATO Chobham armour. The M1's gas turbine engine gives it unequalled acceleration for dashing from cover to cover (tanks do not cruise into combat like squadrons of battleships any more), and there are reports that some, if not all, of the T-80s have a similar engine in place of the usual diesel. Both NATO tanks use a manual loader that experience suggests is more effective than the Soviet's automatic one. NATO thermal night sights for all-weather firing are an important advantage; the T-80 does not have one.

The T-80 may not be revolutionary, but it is still highly effective. The Soviets have shown that they have weapons which, despite their flaws, can be just as good as those deployed by the West. NATO must continue to improve the one area where they are still ahead of the Soviets – tactics and training.

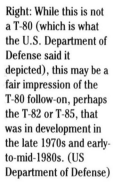

Right: While this is not a T-80 (which is what the U.S. Department of Defense said it depicted), this may be a fair impression of the T-80 follow-on, perhaps the T-82 or T-85, that was in development in the late 1970s and early-to-mid-1980s. (US Department of Defense)

A BTR/60PB dismounts its squad, who must lift themselves through the roof hatches and jump from the vehicle top. (US Navy)

2
70TH MOTORIZED RIFLE BRIGADE, KANDAHAR, AFGHANISTAN

THERE is an old proverb that holds happy the land with no history. In Afghanistan, Kandahar's position at the crossroads of southern Asia, has earned it a long history of armies and traders. Alexander the Great, the last invader who succeeded in conquering the Afghans, let his elephants wallow in the mud flats there before crossing the Indus to complete his conquest of the world. Outside Kandahar in 1878, the Afghans dealt the British Army one of its most painful defeats, at Maiwand. Then, the Afghans brought to the battle not only superior numbers, but high-technology, Victorian style, in the form of breech-loading artillery and repeating rifles. Afghans are quick learners when it comes to weapons.

The Soviet Army came to the city of Kandahar in January 1980, a few days after they had invaded Afghanistan, moving out from the airport – built with American aid funds in the 1950s – where they had had forces deployed since December. The city had risen in open war against the Communist government in 1979, with members of the Army garrison joining with merchants and students. The result had been intense air bombardment of the city itself. After the Soviet invasion, the people rose again, hacking to pieces in traditional Afghan fashion a group of Soviet advisers who had left their compound. In 1980, Kandahar, both bazaar and countryside was, for the Soviets, 'bandit country'. It remains so today.

The Soviets have not tried to pacify Kandahar, any more than they have tried to pacify the Afghan countryside. They occupy the airfield – lengthened in 1981 to accommodate bombers capable of striking in the Persian Gulf – and key government buildings; and their attention is drawn to the countryside only when they need to pass convoys along the roads or need to clear out Afghan villages.

In Kandahar, since 1980, the guarding and clearing has been the business of the Kabul Regime's hapless 12th Division, backed up by the Soviet 70th Motorized Rifle Brigade. The 12th is typical of the divisions of the quisling DRA (Democratic Republic of Afghanistan, which is neither a Democracy, a Republic, nor Afghan, but rather one of the Soviet Union's least successful political creations). The 12th

ORGANIZATION – 70TH MOTORIZED RIFLE BRIGADE

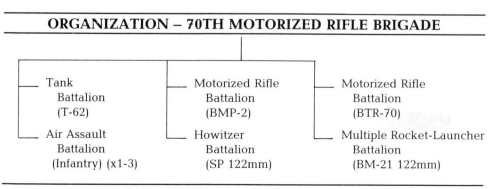

| Tank Battalion (T-62) | Motorized Rifle Battalion (BMP-2) | Motorized Rifle Battalion (BTR-70) |
| Air Assault Battalion (Infantry) (x1-3) | Howitzer Battalion (SP 122mm) | Multiple Rocket-Launcher Battalion (BM-21 122mm) |

Division is the size of a regiment. While sometimes the 12th's khaki-uniformed troopers will fight fiercely against the Resistance, many pass information to the Resistance and seek to desert. The burden of combat in the Kandahar area must fall, then, on the 70th.

The 70th did not come across the border with the motorized rifle divisions that took part in the December 1979 invasion, but was formed in Afghanistan. Many of its personnel apparently came from the 105th Guards Airborne Division on its disbandment. The aggressive paratroopers gave the 70th a hard-fighting reputation. It is one of the few Soviet formations known to the Afghan guerrillas by designation.

MOTORIZED RIFLE TROOPS – THE HEART OF THE ARMY

The 70th Motorized Rifle Brigade is similar to a motorized rifle regiment. It has three, four or more motorized rifle battalions: in the early 1980s, one or more battalion with BMP-1s, one with BMP-2s, one trained for heliborne operations, and possibly one with BTR-APCs (the BTRs might have been for the heliborne battalion). There is also a tank battalion, a BM-21 multiple rocket-launcher battalion and a 122mm howitzer battalion. All of these are organized in much the same way as these units are in motorized rifle divisions.

Although motorized rifle brigades like the 70th are rare in the Soviet order of battle, these independent brigades are believed to be the model for others being formed in new divisions in the Western Military Districts, for independent operations under command of OMG divisions.

Motorized rifle divisions are the most common type of Soviet division. They are, like the 70th, a combined arms formation. Not only do motorized rifle divisions carry the burden of the war in Afghanistan, but they form the bulk of Soviet forces in all theatres.

In combined arms offensives motorized rifle divisions are to be found in the first echelon of Soviet armies. They would be the first to encounter the enemy. Their two BTR-equipped regiments, each with an organic tank battalion, will usually make the initial attack, to be followed up by the

Left: While the 70th Motorized Rifle Brigade uses primarily 5.45mm-calibre infantry weapons, it has upgunned its dismounted firepower with BG-15 40mm grenade launchers, RPG-18 anti-tank rocket launchers, AGS-17 grenade launchers, and PKM 7.62mm general-purpose machine-guns, as carried here by a soldier advancing as part of a squad skirmish line, with a BMP-1 in close support.

ORGANIZATION – TYPICAL MOTORIZED RIFLE DIVISION GROUP SOVIET FORCES GERMANY

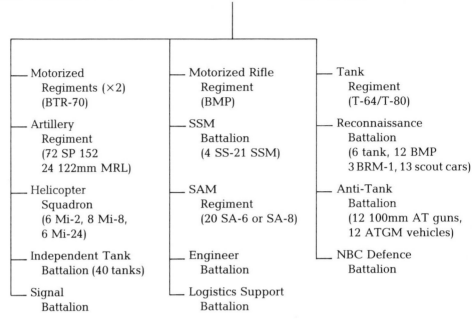

Left: An AGS-17 30mm grenade launcher. This weapon has upgunned the firepower of Soviet motorized rifle sub-units in the 1970s and 1980s and has been extensively used in action in Afghanistan. (US Department of Defense)

BMP COMPANY IN THE ATTACK WITH TANK PLATOON

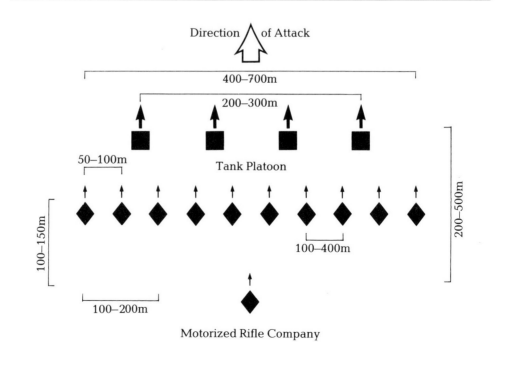

Left: BMP-1s demonstrate their ability to make diesel smoke from their engines. (US Navy)

70TH MOTORIZED RIFLE BRIGADE

MEN	3–4,000
T-62 Tanks	40
BMP-2 IFVs	36
BTR-70 APCs	37
122mm SP Howitzer M-1974 2S1	24
BM-21 122mm MRL	24
RPG-16 AT Weapon	105
AGS-17 Grenade-launcher	18
RPK-74 5.45mm LMG	81

TYPICAL MOTORIZED RIFLE DIVISION GROUP SOVIET FORCES GERMANY

MEN	13,800
T-64 or T-80 Tanks	277
BMP-1 or BMP-2/IFV	142
BTR-60PB/BTR-70/BTR-80	290
BRM or BRM-7 recon vehicles	19
BRDM-2 scout cars	29
152mm SP howitzer M-1974 2S3	72
122mm SP howitzer M-1973 2S1	96
BM-21 122mm MRL	24
SS-21 surface-to-surface missile-launcher	4
SA-6 or SA-8 SP SAM launcher	20
SA-13 SP SAM launcher	16
ZSU-23-4 SP AA gun	16
BRDM-2 SP ATGM launcher	39
T-12A 100mm AT guns	12
Mi-2 Hoplite light helicopter	6
Mi-8 Hip medium helicopter	8
Mi-24 Hind-E attack helicopter	6
SA-7 or SA-14 SAM launcher	120
RPG-16 AT weapon	598
AGS-17 30mm grenade-launcher	54
RPK-74 5.45mm LMG	508

BMP-equipped motorized rifle regiment and the division's tank regiment. These, too, could be in the first echelon of a motorized rifle division, but one or both of these regiments would probably be in the division's second echelon.

Once the motorized rifle division has thrown its weight into an attack, and committed its first echelon and then its second echelon regiments to battle, it should have broken through what the Soviets define as the tactical depths of the defence. Then the Soviets can move through the gap with either a tank division or another motorized rifle division from the army's second echelon, or an operational manoeuvre group, starting the exploitation or the pursuit.

The importance of motorized rifle troops is seen throughout the Soviet Army. The Russians' belief in the tank has not blinded them to the fact that tanks cannot survive without motorized rifle troops and artillery fighting with them. They suppress the anti-tank weapons that have the potential for decimating armoured forces.

The Soviets have not only aimed at having one BMP-equipped motorized rifle regiment in each tank and motorized rifle division, but also one BMP-equipped motorized rifle battalion in each tank regiment, increasing combined-arms integration. The tank and the BMP are basic building blocks of Soviet mechanized combat forces.

THE BMP – FROM AFGHANISTAN TO EUROPE

The BMPs which the 70th use to protect convoys on the dusty, cratered roads of

Above left: The troopers of the 70th use the 5.45mm RPK-74 light machine-gun as their standard squad automatic weapon. It can be fired through the

orward gunports on ach side of a BMP. The oviet Army, like the ritish and American, as moved away from aving 7.62mm-calibre eneral-purpose nachine-guns at squad r section level. (US epartment of Defense)

ight: A line of BMP-1s without ATGMs nounted – advances, naking smoke from heir diesel engines to over the vehicles ehind them.

elow: BMP-1s and notorized rifle troops in vinter terrain.

Afghanistan, where every rock seems to conceal a pair of hostile eyes, were designed for quite another type of war. In the late 1950s and early 1960s, the Soviets started looking for a way to employ motorized rifle troops on a battlefield dominated by nuclear, biological, and chemical weapons. Then, the Soviet view was that any future war in Europe would begin with a massive nuclear strike, followed by a high-speed advance by tank-heavy forces. The BMP had a NBC defence system, could go anywhere a T-62 tank could go, and had a tank-killing capability in its 73mm cannon and a *Sagger* ATGM. The motorized riflemen would not even need to dismount to fight. firing through gunports in the side of the troop compartment.

The BMP first entered wide-scale service in 1967, about the same time as the Soviets decided that they would try and become capable of fighting either a nuclear or a conventional war in Europe. The BMP (and the improved BMP-1, introduced in about 1970) became more important because it was an already available system while the Soviets looked, in the mid-1970s, for new tactics that could prevail against increasingly accurate battlefield weapons, such as ATGMs and tanks equipped with laser rangefinders.

Lessons of the Middle East fighting,

Below: Dismounted assault! Motorized rifle troops use marching fire from their 5.45mm calibre weapons. These BMP-1s will not only use their 73mm cannon and machine-guns, but will also be supported by main battle tanks. (US Navy)

together with large-scale Soviet exercises, provided raw material for this tactical evolution. The heavy losses suffered by both Israeli and Arab tank units in the 1973 war further demonstrated the need for cooperation with motorized rifle troops and artillery. The Soviets realized that if their idea of a mass, mechanized, combined arms army was not to be invalidated by new weapons, they would have to make some changes in hardware, in tactics, in operations, and in organization, all involving the BMP.

BMP's armament has improved. By the mid-70s, the joystick guidance system of the BMP's Sagger ATGM had been re-

placed by a more modern system, where the gunner only has to keep the target in the crosshairs. In the late 1970s and early 1980s, the Sagger was replaced by the more modern Spigot system, a copy of the NATO Milan. The BMP-2 entered service in the late 1970s. It mounts a 30mm automatic cannon which, while it lacks the 73mm's tank-killing capability, is more effective against targets such as the 20mm-armed Marder infantry fighting vehicle which would perforate the BMP before its slower firing weapon could be on target.

The BMP gives the Soviets tactical dynamism. BMP-equipped companies and battalions, called 'Forward detachments', will push ahead of the Soviet advance guards to take key road junctions, choke-points, bridges, linking up with para-troopers and heliborne forces. They will also raid headquarters, communications sites and act, as the Soviets write, as 'the keys that unlock the stability of the defence'.

Operationally, BMPs make possible the combined arms mobility of Soviet deep offensives in Europe, southern Asia, or China. The combination of mobility and fire-power that the individual BMP provides becomes even more significant when *en masse* and in combination with tanks, artillery, air defence, helicopters, and improved logistics. The BMP's influence on the Soviet Army stretches far beyond the troubled walls of ancient Kandahar.

THE 70TH MOTORIZED RIFLE BRIGADE IN ACTION

The 70th is not only a combined arms formation, but is capable of carrying out a wide range of tactics. The motorized rifle battalion, which is trained in heliborne assaults, is used for the type of tactics that have increasingly characterized Soviet operations since 1984. The other motorized rifle battalions, supported by the tanks and artillery, take part in combined arms mechanized offensives and escort the convoys of hundreds of trucks which run between Kandahar, Kabul and Herat two or three times a week.

Convoy escort is a major role of all Soviet mechanized forces in Afghanistan, and few convoys arrive without having encountered at least one guerrilla ambush. Some of these develop into pitched battles and the convoys do not always get through. In March 1984, guerrillas from the Panjsher Valley burned 25 fuel tractor-trailers on the long upgrade to the Salang Pass tunnel which the guerrillas call 'the Suez Canal'. The Salang route – it runs direct from Kabul to the Soviet Union – was blocked for weeks.

The war the 70th is fighting has reasons more apparent to the men in the Kremlin than to the men in the BMPs. The Soviets do not want a Moscow-approved Marxist-Leninist government to fall to Islamic guerrillas, nor do they wish to give up the geopolitical leverage and potential for military action against Pakistan, Iran and the Gulf. Airfields in southern Afghanistan provide bases for Soviet bombers within 400 air miles of the Strait of Hormuz and the West's petroleum lifelines.

Until 1983, many of the 70th's personnel were sent to their units after initial induction. While specialists went through three to six month courses in USSR-based training divisions, the units in Afghanistan used

INFANTRY FIGHTING VEHICLES

	BMP-1	BMD-1		BMP-1	BMD-1
Crew	3 (cdr, driver, gunner)	3 (cdr, driver gunner)	Infra-red:		
			Driver	yes	yes
			Gunner	yes	no
Passenger			Commander	yes	yes
capacity	8	4	NBC Protection	filtration &	filtration &
Weight (mt)	13.5	7.5		over-	over-
Ground				pressure	pressure
Presssure				system	system
(kg/cm^2)	0.57	0.57	Gun calibre		
Length (gun			(mm)	73	73
forward) (m)	6.74	5.41	Type	smoothbore	smoothbore
Width, overall			Traverse	360°	360°
(m)	2.94	2.55	Elevation	−4°−+33°	−4°−+33°
Height,			Rate of fire (rpm)		
overall (m)	2.15	1.77	(Maximum/		
Clearance (mm)	400	100–450	Sustained)	8/2–3	8/2–3
Engine	V-6, 290hp, diesel	V-6, 240hp, diesel	Stabilization	no	no
			Ammunition		
Max. speed:			(type)	HEAT-FS,	HEAT-FS,
Road (km/hr)	70	80		Frag-HE	Frag-HE
Water (km/hr)	6	10		(FS)	(FS)
Fuel Capacity			Muzzle Velocity (m/s):		
(litres)	460	300	HEAT-FS	700	700
Road Range			FRAG-HE (FS)	700	700
(km)	500	320	Max. range (m)	2,200	2,200
Trench Crossing			Effective range,		
(m)	2.00	1.60	50% Ph (m)	800	800
Vertical Step			Armour	300	300
(m)	0.80	0.80	Penetration	(HEAT-	(HEAT-
Max. gradient	30°	32°	(mm @ 0°	FS	FS
Fording (m)	amphibious	amphibious	obliquity	any	any
Armour			00/1,000m)	range)	range)
(maximum):			Basic load (rd)	40	40
Hull (mm)	19	15	Secondary		
Turret (mm)	23	25	armament	1×7.62mm	3×7.62mm
			ATGM launcher	1	1

Above: BTR-60PBs in the snow. The BTR-60PB and its follow-on, the BTR-70, constitute the most numerous Soviet armoured vehicles in Afghanistan. The 70th probably has one battalion in BTRs. Even the Afghanistan-based air assault brigade, the 56th, reportedly has enough BTRs for one battalion.

Right: A BMP-2 of the
70th Motorized Rifle
Brigade in Afghanistan,
showing its long-
barrelled 30mm gun.

to have to train most of their bi-annual intake of conscripts themselves and then use them in combat. When their two years of service were completed, they were sent home. Before this, the personnel situation was even worse. During the 1979 invasion and early 1980, most of the men of the motorized rifle divisions committed to action in Afghanistan were recalled reservists from the Turkestan and Central Asia Military Districts. Often poorly trained and never having been mobilized before as part of these divisions, most were Muslims and had little enthusiasm for killing their brethren. By 1984, however, the Soviets had started to send all troops destined for Afghanistan through training courses in the Soviet Union lasting three to six months.

This improved level of training is one reason why the Soviet deployment has improved since their early set-backs. The Afghans say the Soviets are becoming progressively more adept, especially since early 1984. Not only are the BMP crews of the 70th learning, but the men in Moscow as well.

THE SOVIET ARMY FIGHTS ITS WAR

Mao Tse-tung wrote, 'The guerrilla must move among the people as a fish swims in the sea.' The Soviets are not trying to catch the fish one at a time, they are draining the ocean. Not attempting to occupy the countryside of Afghanistan, they are content to hold the cities and airfields, and keep control of the roads. To secure these they are depopulating large areas of the countryside, near the roads, in food-producing areas, or along infiltration routes from Pakistan.

The Soviets have had great difficulty in adapting to a guerrilla war. Until 1984, they were unable to take advantage of guerrilla inexperience, seldom moved on high ground, or practised aggressive small unit tactics. Even by 1987, most motorized rifle units mounted in BTRs or BMPs remain road-bound with limited tactical flexibility. To compensate, the Soviets make lavish use of artillery, fixed-wing fighter-bombers or, the most important single weapons system in the war, heli-

copters, especially Hind attack helicopters. The use of Stinger and Blowpipe SAMs by the Resistance in 1987 has, however, greatly hindered Soviet air power.

This is why the 70th's heliborne battalion is significant. The helicopter also supplies mobility. The Soviets have been using these forces, together with *Spetsnaz* (special operations groups), for unconventional warfare, in ambush patrols along infiltration routes and for extended dismounted operations into Afghan-controlled areas.

The 70th, like all Soviet formations, must be capable of operating under chemical warfare conditions. There is clear and convincing evidence of the Soviet use of chemical weapons in Afghanistan. The weapons used include older gases such as phosgene, CS, and CN as well as standard nerve agents and new high-technology agents. This requires NBC training and decontamination, although the pattern of Soviet use of chemical weapons in Afghanistan remains limited and inconsistent.

The 70th has lost more than a few comrades in battle. By 1987, the Soviets were estimated to have lost more than 15,000 killed in action with three times as many wounded. Hepatitis and other diseases have also taken their toll.

THE BATTLE OF ZHAWAR, 1986

The border fighting of 1986, while having interdiction of guerrilla movement and resupply as a primary mission, was also apparently intended to increase political pressure on Iran and Pakistan. The Soviets decided to interdict guerrilla supply routes without having to maintain a presence on the ground, or having to mount an air anti-infiltration campaign on the US model. Minelaying was backed up by increased efforts by special forces and helicopters.

In April, the Soviets launched a major offensive into Paktia province on the border with Pakistan. The target was Zhawar, the base (*markaz*) of Jalluladin Haqani, a *maulawi* (religious teacher) of the *Hezb-i-Islami* party of Younis Khalis, one of the seven major parties of the Afghan Resistance. Jalluladin had

Right: Afghanistan. (US Department of State)

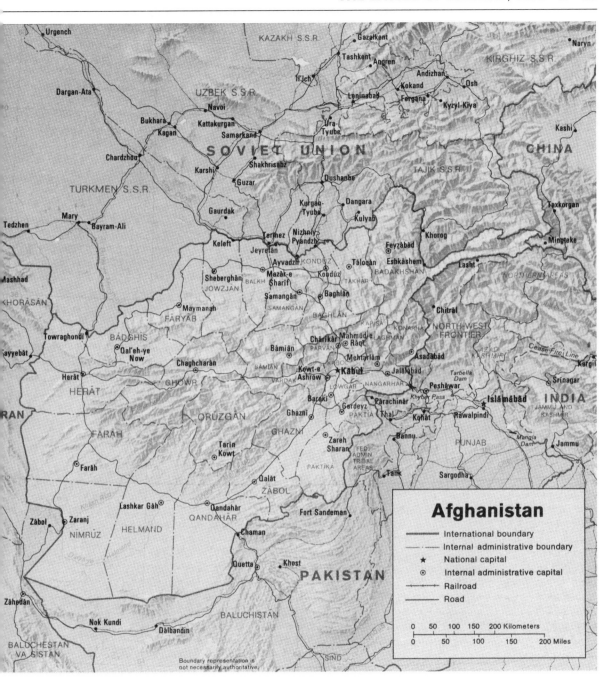

emerged, in 1985, as the leading resistance commander in all Paktia province.

As much for prestige as for logistics, Jalluladin had built a considerable base at Zhawar. Since the Afghans have obtained more and heavier weapons, and because the Soviet scorched earth tactics mean that the Resistance usually cannot live off the land, increasingly ammunition and food need to be brought into the interior by truck and pack animal. This means creating storage caches for use while convoys are organized – as at Zhawar. Zhawar not only had weapons caches and supply dumps, but generators and billets. Nestling in a deep valley, its defences were strong. Jalluladin's fighting men were border Pathans, whose ancestors were vividly depicted by Kipling. Among the anti-aircraft defences were three Bofors guns,

Left: The 70th's erstwhile allies, the Democratic Republic of Afghanistan Army, in action firing a Soviet 82mm mortar. These troops will often try and switch sides if given the opportunity; at other times, however, the DRA forces will fight ferociously against the Resistance.

positioned so that any Hind helicopter that probed the valley would end up with a 40mm hole for easy ventilation through the cockpit.

The Soviets also had prestige at stake at Zhawar. They needed to show the Resistance, their DRA allies, and the world that Communist forces could still go anywhere in Afghanistan. The Zhawar offensive differed from those of the previous year in that the Soviets did not carry the burden of the offensive themselves. Rather, they left it to their erstwhile Afghan Communist allies. The DRA Army, to show it could fight, was committed to the offensive. Elements of the 12th, 14th and 25th Infantry Divisions were sent into action, as was the 37th Commando Brigade. DRA militia forces also participated, including Khost and Jadji tribal militias. But the Soviets were not sending this force into action without their advisers, present at every headquarters down to battalion level. The heavy ground punch was provided by the Soviets as well. A brigade-sized force backed up the Communist Afghans, either the 70th from Kandahar or a force from the 103rd Guards Airborne Division in Kabul. Above them were large numbers of fighter-bombers and Hind attack helicopters.

Using their targeting information, painstakingly built up from agents, air reconnaissance and radio intercepts, the Soviets launched days of intense airstrikes and long-range artillery fire, with heavy use of 122mm multiple rocket-launchers. This preliminary barrage was perhaps more suited to the 1945 drive on Berlin than to guerrilla conflict, but while wasteful of ammunition, it had the effect of keeping many of the Resistance in caves and shelters and not moving up to ambush positions on the ridge-lines.

The basic thrust was hardly imaginative; the troops slowly fought their way through the valley that ran like a corridor towards Zhawar. But the Soviets were not going to simply let the DRA drift towards the objective. Helicopter-borne special operations forces were lifted in to take the high ground and to ambush Resistance reinforcements. When these operations were carried out by well-trained Soviet heliborne forces – possibly including a battalion of the 70th – they were successful.

When the DRA tried to carry out similar operations, they were less so. The 37th Commando Brigade, one of the DRA's 'hard-luck' units, was again ambushed as it tried to land in Hip helicopters near Zhawar.

But the day turned against the Resistance. Perhaps emboldened by their additional weaponry and mindful of the fact that hard stand-and-fight tactics had caused the Soviets to turn back short of their goal during the 1985 offensive to relieve Khost, the Afghans did not fade away when confronted at Zhawar. Rather,

Right: The threat to the 70th – an Afghan guerrilla armed with an RPG-7 anti-tank grenade launcher. RPG-7s and mines have accounted for most of the Soviet armoured fighting vehicles lost in Afghanistan. (Committee for a Free Afghanistan, Washington, DC)

ght: What the 70th
es to prevent – the
termath of a guerrilla
nbush. The Afghans
ll strip the knocked-
t trucks for anything
value. (Committee for
Free Afghanistan,
ashington, DC)

they matched their 107mm rockets, SA-7s and RPG-7s against the Soviets. Losses were heavy on both sides. At least seven Soviet and Afghan Communist helicopters and fighter-bombers went down, possibly more. It may be that the Soviets wanted a conventional-style battle, where their air-power and superior firepower would be most effective, and were using the push on Zhawar to draw the guerrillas into the open.

The 70th may never reach the anti-guerrilla skill of British forces in Malaya or French forces in Algeria, but Zhawar showed it to be adequate for what the Soviets had in mind. Even the DRA Army – many of whose soldiers have no love for the Communists and will desert at the first opportunity – actually carried out their mission. The Communists took Zhawar at the end of April 1986, but made no attempt to hold it. After destroying everything they pulled out and left the ruins to the guerrillas.

In 1987, the Soviets found the success of Zhawar – fleeting as successes often are in counter-insurgency warfare – difficult to repeat. The Stingers and Blowpipes have greatly raised the cost of the war on the battlefield. The massed airstrikes of Zhawar have given way to less accurate high altitude bombing; helicopters found themselves greatly limited in 1987. In May-June 1987, at Agrandhab, near Kandahar, the DRA 12th Division launched an attack, backed up by the 70th, and was soundly defeated. At the same time, Soviet troops had to make the next large scale offensive into Paktia, at Jaji, and despite the presence of large numbers of airborne and air assault troopers, the Soviets were also defeated. DRA morale started to crack. Soviet morale, aggravated by the poor conditions of service is often low. If the Soviet leadership moves to end the war, it will be, in large part, because the Afghans have made it more costly to continue it.

Right: Soviet armour runs into trouble in Afghanistan – a knocked out T-55 main battle tank with the Afghan guerrillas who knocked it out. (US Information Agency)

Below: A Soviet artillery battery in action – equipped with 130mm M-46 M-1954 field guns. They are dug into open gun pits. The Soviets now place less emphasis on digging in artillery, instead deploying them over a greater area to avoid counter-battery fire. The accurate, long-range M-46 is now being replaced by SP and towed 152mm field guns, but has seen much combat and is still in widespread Soviet service.

3

34TH GUARDS ARTILLERY DIVISION, POTSDAM, EAST GERMANY

IF there were to be a European temple to Mars, Potsdam would be an appropriate site. It was there in the eighteenth century that King Frederick William exalted close-order drill from battlefield necessity to national ritual. His son, Frederick the Great, found the Age of Reason not incompatible with finding better ways to march his Prussian grenadiers to the battlefield. At Potsdam first sprouted the German way of war. Its latest blossomings can be seen there as the long, stone-grey convoys of *National Volksarmee* pass, their spotlessly clean Soviet-made trucks keeping the precise 50-metre intervals that seem to elude their allies of the Group Soviet Forces, Germany. The East German Army remains very much a German Army.

There is no single country that has had as great an influence on the course of Russian and Soviet military thought as Germany. When European ideas were needed to leaven the strong bread of the Russian way of war, it came from Germany. Indeed, Clausewitz himself did some of his best service in Russian uniform.

But foreign ideas from Germany, or elsewhere, had to deal with Russian reality. Russia – today as in the past – has lots of peasants. There has seldom been enough money in the Kremlin treasury to keep all the peasants well trained at arms, either Muscovite levies or today's reservists, who receive much less regular refresher training than their US or British counterparts.

To stiffen the brave if unpractised men in the front lines, a solution has been, since the time of Ivan the Terrible, to field large amounts of heavy artillery, manned, if not by professional gunners, by those able to serve the guns under the eye of those whose technical knowledge – often from abroad – could create an effective force. Russian artillery held the front line against Napoleon at Borodino and against the Germans at Tannenberg, even when the infantry would not stand. During the Second World War, Soviet artillery inflicted half of all the battlefield casualties suffered by the German Army in the East.

The barracks at Potsdam are home to more than Prussian memories, but also to the flagship of Soviet artillery, the 34th Guards Artillery Division. With four brigades of artillery, the 34th represents Group Soviet Forces, Germany's most concentrated and farthest-reaching source of conventional ground firepower.

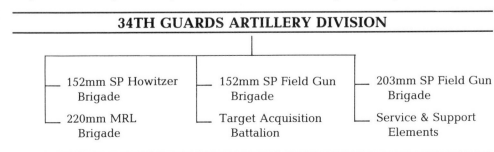

34TH GUARDS ARTILLERY DIVISION

— 152mm SP Howitzer Brigade

— 220mm MRL Brigade

— 152mm SP Field Gun Brigade

— Target Acquisition Battalion

— 203mm SP Field Gun Brigade

— Service & Support Elements

THE 34TH AND SOVIET ARTILLERY

It was a maxim in the Soviet Army of the Second World War that 'Artillery kills. Infantry dies.' The Soviets know that artillery is the biggest casualty-causer in modern war. It is the most efficient way to deliver firepower on the battlefield. Artillery is far enough to the rear to make ammunition resupply much easier than for the mortars up with the front-line troops. Artillery is more responsive and cheaper than aircraft. The Soviets will never use bombs where they can use shells.

Artillery may lack the glamour of tanks or helicopters, but it is a fundamental element in the Soviet equation for victory in any future war in Europe. Equations play a large part in Soviet thinking about artillery, and artillery is by its nature suited to the Soviet predilection for applying scientific principles to war. Detailed plans, charts and nomograms of effectiveness characterize much of the Soviet Army's operations and tactics, but never more so than when dealing with artillery.

The 34th, in wartime, would probably split into two divisions, one to each of the

34TH GUARDS ARTILLERY DIVISION

MEN	7,000
152mm SP howitzer M-1974 2S3	72–96
152mm SP field gun M-1976 2S5	72–96
203mm SP field gun M-1975 2S7	72–96
220mm multiple rocket-launcher BM-27	72

two *fronts* (roughly equivalent to Western army groups, with two armies and eight or more divisions) that Group Soviet Forces, Germany would probably deploy. The heavy artillery found in the 34th would be used to form Army Artillery Groups (AAGs). These are task-organized groups of artillery battalions under the command of each army (roughly equivalent to a Western corps or army with three to four divisions) which will be used for long-range general-support fire missions, including counter-battery and interdiction.

The Soviets are not looking to repeat the hub-to-hub artillery deployments of so many of their successful 'Patriotic War' offensives. Those concentrations would present vulnerable targets to either nuclear or conventional weapons, and

Left: While self-
propelled artillery equips
the divisions in East
Germany, the standard
divisional weapon in
most of the Soviet Army
remains the 122mm
D-30 M-1963 howitzer. It
is also used by the
Guards Airborne
Divisions. (US Navy)

Below: A Soviet 122mm
D-74 field gun – an
example captured by the
U.S. Marine Corps in
Vietnam – that
represents part of the
earlier 'long reach' of
Soviet forces in East
Germany.

degrade the speed and surprise which the Soviets value so highly. Rather, the Soviets will look towards manoeuvre by fire. The AAGs drawn from the regiments of the 34th would be dispersed and mobile, for to be otherwise in the face of modern weapons is to be dead. Fire would be concentrated from different battalions with the aid of new technology. The 34th already has digital computers at battalion and higher levels. Target acquisition can be by radars (such as the long-ranged *Big Fred*), forward command observation posts (equipped with laser rangefinders) or even spotting carried out by behind-the-lines *Spetsnaz* commandos. The long reach requires a long view.

The 34th is not all burnished steel and clinking breechblocks. It is made up of men; and Group Soviet Forces, Germany must make the best of the 19-year-old conscripts it receives every six months, some (always, it must seem to the 34th's officers, too few) with six months' specialist training. Others may be only 30 days off the *kolkhoz*.

This twice-annual rotation, in which the 34th, like every Soviet division in East Germany, loses the most experienced quarter of its conscripts at the end of their two years' service in exchange for a fresh intake, is one of NATO's most important warning indicators. If ever the new recruits arrive, but the time-expired men do not board Aeroflot for home, it is time for Europe to look to its guns.

Not only must the 34th train its conscripts, but every season it must send a contingent to help gather the harvest in the Ukraine – another indicator for NATO if omitted. Even with its world-class weapons and high technology, the 34th cannot escape the black hole of the Soviet economy.

The 34th's officers fare better. Its command is probably the plum major-general's billet in the Soviet Army's artillery. Group Soviet Forces, Germany has been the 'fast track' to advancement in the Soviet Army because, as the cutting edge of the entire Soviet war machine, its senior officers are hand-picked.

■ THE STALIN ORGAN

When the Germans invaded the Soviet Union on 22 June 1941, the Soviet Army had precisely eight multiple rocket-launchers. Hardly an auspicious start for what was to prove one of the war's most effective artillery systems, but Soviet industry soon rushed them into large-scale production, the first multiple rocket-launchers going into action in July 1941, on the Smolensk Front.

The Germans received many unpleasant surprises when they invaded Russia. They found that the country was even bigger than it looked on the map, that the roads were even worse than they looked on the map, and they found the multiple rocket-launcher. They called it the 'Stalin Organ' – they thought it looked like a pipe instrument, and joked that things were so bad they were being stripped out of the Kremlin. The jokes stopped when the first rockets arrived.

One of the tactical strengths of multiple rocket-launchers is that the first projectiles on target from any artillery piece are always the most effective ones; troops have only a few seconds to dash for cover. While an artillery piece can put only one projectile into the air at a time, a multiple rocket-launcher can fire all its rockets within seconds, and they arrive as one salvo. The MRL is an ideal area-fire weapon.

The main Soviet multiple rocket-launcher of the 'Patriotic War', 16-round 132mm BM-13, is still in action in the hands of the quisling Democratic Republic of Afghanistan Army, evidence of the soundness of its design. Throughout the war, the Soviets found that the multiple rocket-launcher fitted their style of fighting. It was cheap and easy to build – after all, it was only a truck with metal launch rails – so large numbers could be deployed. Being an area weapon, it did not require pinpoint accuracy as, unlike today, Soviet artillery fire control was not capable of pinpoint accuracy during much of the Second World War.

The multiple rocket-launcher is not a replacement for tube artillery; it is basically an offensive weapon. It takes longer to reload than standard tube artillery and thus cannot react to rapidly changing situations. This severely restricts its use for defensive fire. The rockets themselves cost more to produce than artillery shells, and are bulkier and more difficult to transport.

The Soviets began to develop new multiple rocket-launchers in the 1950s, replacing the wartime types. The 132mm weapons were joined by the 140mm BM-14, the 240mm BM-24 and the 200mm BMD-200. The most numerically important post-war Soviet multiple rocket-launcher, however, was the 122mm BM-21, introduced in 1964.

Above left: The 140mm 16-tube BM-14 multiple rocket-launcher was the standard Soviet divisional MRL before the introduction of the BM-21. It is still in use in the Soviet Union and abroad.

Above right: The 140mm BM-14 multiple rocket-launcher, shown here in its towed 12-tube version, was used by Soviet Guards Airborne Divisions until replaced by a lightened truck-mounted version of the BM-21.

Right: A 122mm BM-21 multiple rocket-launcher. While replaced in the 34th Guards Artillery Division by the BM-27, the BM-21 remains the standard divisional multiple rocket launcher. (US Army)

THE BM-21

Today, the BM-21 remains the standard Soviet divisional multiple rocket-launcher. Each Soviet tank and motorized rifle division, of which there are about 180, has a battalion of 18–24 multiple rocket-launchers, usually BM-21s (although some low-readiness divisions may still have older equipment). In addition, many Soviet tank and motorized regiments – of which each division has four – will receive six GRAD-1 36-barrel versions of the BM-21

on mobilization. The BM-21 equipped the 34th's 72-launcher multiple rocket-launcher brigade before it re-equipped with heavier weapons.

A primary BM-21 mission is delivering chemical weapons. Multiple rocket-launchers can deliver large concentrations of chemical rounds instantaneously, rather than having a slower build-up to toxic quantities as with howitzers. One BM-21 battalion salvo can create lethal concentrations of blood-agent chemicals over an area greater than two square kilometres.

The Soviets often co-locate BM-21 units with radio direction-finding facilities. Soviet radio direction-finding nets with ten stations can find the position of a tactical radio within 30 seconds and with only a degree of error that is less than the area covered by a battery volley from six BM-21s – 240 high-explosive or chemical rockets. The rockets will be on target within three minutes of the initial intercept.

MULTIPLE ROCKET-LAUNCHERS

	122mm (40-rounds) **BM-21**	220mm (16-rounds) **BM-27**
Introduced	1964	1977
Elevation	0°–+75°	0°–+55°
Traverse	180°	240°
Calibre (mm)	122	220
Weight (kg)	66.0	300
Length (m)	2.87	4.8
Type of stabilization	fin & spin	fin & spin
Max. range (km)	20.3	35
Warhead (types)	Frag-HE, chemical, smoke, incendiary	Frag-HE, chemical, scatterable, mines, incendiary
Unit of Fire (rd)	120	32
Emplacement time launcher pre-loaded (min)	2.5	2.0
Displacement time (min)	0.5	0.5
Crew	5	8
Model	Ural-375D (6×6)	ZiL-135 (8×8)
Weight (kg)	13,300	23,000
Length (m)	7.35	9.3
Width (m)	2.69	2.8
Height (m)	2.89	3.2
Max. road speed (km/hr)	75	65
Fuel capacity (litres)	360	770
Road range (km)	750	520

[1]Travel position.

The BM-21 is normally mounted on a URAL-375 truck chassis – a standard Soviet tactical truck. The 122mm rocket is a single-stage, solid-fuel design, stabilized by spring-loaded fins which pop up after they are launched. The 36-tube version of the BM-21 is mounted on a lighter ZiL-130 tactical truck, and a 12-tube version is carried on a light GAZ-66 truck for use by Guards Airborne Divisions, replacing an earlier towed version of the 140mm multiple rocket-launcher.

▮ THE MULTIPLE ROCKET-LAUNCHER IN COMBAT

Starting in 1986, the Afghan Resistance has made increasing use of the BM-21's rocket mounted in light-weight metal firing tubes, supplementing the similar but smaller Chinese-designed 107mm rockets previously used. It is much easier to destroy a helicopter or fighter-bomber on the ground at its airbase than shooting it down when it is capable of shooting back. The Afghans previously had to attack Soviet airbases in Afghanistan with short-ranged weapons such as RPG-7 rocket-propelled anti-tank grenade-launchers or 82mm mortars. The Soviets themselves have used multiple rocket-launchers in action in Afghanistan, mainly BM-21s, and the 220mm BM-27. One type of rocket that has reportedly been fired from BM-21s contains a number of incendiary white phosphorous sub-munitions, called 'fire-sticks' by the Afghans.

In 1987, the Soviets increased their use of long range artillery, especially multiple rocket launchers, in Afghanistan to compensate for the increased limits on the use of airpower imposed by improved Afghan air defenses. More BM-27 battalions – called 'BM-41s' by the Afghans because of their estimated range – went into action.

Standard truck-mounted as well as the guerrilla single-tube versions of multiple rocket-launchers were also used in Vietnam and throughout Southeast Asia: BM-21s, 140mm BM-14s, and Chinese-made 107mm versions on a towed mounting.

Soviet multiple rocket-launchers have been used by both sides in the Middle East Wars. In sub-Saharan Africa the BM-21

Right: Aiming an MRL. With his officer supervising, a Soviet gunner sights in his 122mm BM-21 multiple rocket-launcher. (US Army)

Right: A 220mm BM-27 multiple rocket-launcher. Equipping one brigade of the 34th Guards Artillery Division, it is currently the most advanced Soviet multiple rocket-launcher design, although a 280mm calibre follow-on is reported in development. (US Army)

The 34th in action – an artist's impression of a battery of BM-27s opening fire. (US Department of Defense)

has often been spectacularly effective; its noise and explosion has frequently made it a psychologically decisive weapon. Cuban BM-21s in Angola panicked UNITA forces in 1976. The Tanzanians used BM-21s effectively against Idi Amin's forces in the 1976 invasion of Uganda. Both sides had Soviet-built multiple rocket-launchers during the Egypt-Libya fighting of 1977 and in the Ogaden fighting between Somalia and Ethiopia, where, in 1977, Cuban BM-21s proved crucial in gaining a victory for the Soviet-backed Ethiopians.

THE BM-27 – THE 34TH'S LONG REACH

The 34th Guards Artillery Division's 72-launcher multiple rocket-launcher brigade has been equipped, since the early 1980s, with the newest and most effective Soviet mutliple rocket-launcher, which would enable the Soviets to 'strike deep' into NATO tactical-level objectives. The BM-27 has a longer range than any other Soviet artillery weapon, and is a counter to the US-designed MLRS Multiple Launcher Rocket System coming into service throughout NATO.

In addition to the high-explosive and chemical warheads, the BM-27's 220mm rocket also uses fragmentation, incendiary, or minelet submunitions. The big, cross-country ZiL-135 truck chassis is used for the platform for the 220mm MRL, as it is for the separate, dedicated reload vehicle, with an automatic power loading device that accompanies each firing vehicle. The self-contained crane on the reload vehicle also allows for relatively rapid reloading.

BM-27s are deployed in battalions consisting of one HQ, one support, and three firing batteries. Each firing battery has six launcher vehicles and twelve resupply vehicles. Four BM-27-equipped battalions are found in the multiple rocket-launcher brigade of the 34th and probably in the multiple rocket-launcher regiment of army-level artillery brigades as well, replacing BM-21s in these units. The BM-27 will not replace the divisional or regimental BM-21s.

Chemical weapons are a key part of Soviet tactics. During the First World War, Russian troops, often without proper protective equipment or training, suffered proportionately the worst from gas of any combatant army. The Red Army has no desire to repeat the experience. Even Hitler's Germany was deterred from chemical weapons use on the Eastern Front, in part, by the fear of Soviet retaliation. In 1945, captured German nerve gas technology gave the Soviet offensive chemical warfare a new cutting edge. For many years NATO ignored the chemical threat, but in the mid-1970s started to make extensive efforts at improving defensive provisions against a Soviet chemical threat.

The Soviet emphasis on chemical warfare has been reflected in the use not only of chemical weapons in Afghanistan, but by Soviet-supplied armies elsewhere, such as the Egyptians in Yemen in the 1960s and the Vietnamese in Laos and Cambodia in the 1970s and 1980s. Soviet offensive chemical weapons that could be delivered by the 34th's multiple rocket-launchers and tube artillery is not limited to the 1950s-technology nerve agent which makes up the limited NATO stocks of offensive chemical weapons – and only the United States and France hold limited stocks of that. The Soviets probably have stocks of tricothecne toxin 'yellow rain', which has proven highly lethal in Afghanistan. They possibly have new, fast-acting nerve agents, much more deadly than any of the chemists's nightmares that have ever emerged from Western laboratories. There is also strong evidence that the Soviets have developed an effective non-lethal incapacitant agent. Widespread use of this on the battlefield could make it an effective weapon of suppression while not opening the door to further escalation.

The NATO MLRS is similar to the BM-27, but more sophisticated. It is doubtful whether the Soviet weapon has the on-vehicle communications and fire-control equipment. Rather, fire control and communications would be handled by the battery and battalion command vehicles, which means that it is unlikely that BM-27s will be employed on roving, independent, responsive fire missions in the way that MLRSs can be used. Similarly, NATO is currently working on guided submunitions for the MLRS round. The Soviets are unlikely to be advanced enough in state-

BM-27 MRL BATTERY FIRING POSITION

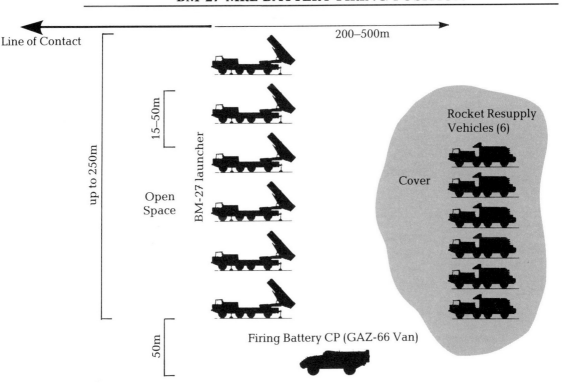

Line of Contact

200–500m

up to 250m

15–50m

BM-27 launcher

Open Space

50m

Firing Battery CP (GAZ-66 Van)

Rocket Resupply Vehicles (6)

Cover

of-the-art guidance technology to develop a comparable capability for the BM-27 in the near future. The BM-27 may lack the sophistication of the MLRS, but it is long-ranged. All Soviet multiple rocket-launchers are unarmoured, and are vulnerable if caught in the open, so quick, responsive counter-battery fire, by systems employing area-coverage weapons, is still as effective against multiple rocket-launchers as it was during the Second World War.

THE 34TH AND THE DEEP BATTLE

The introduction of the BM-27 during the period 1976–77 meshed with the Soviets' renewed emphasis on the use of Operational Manoeuvre Groups and the organization of *front*-level Air Assault and Airmobile Brigades. It is part of the Soviet Army's new 'fight deep' capability. Here again, changing hardware reflects the Soviet desire to have new battlefield capabilities. The BM-27s are excellent wea-

pons for concentrating massed fire on key targets. This is important because the Soviets see the increasing lethality of modern battlefield weapons – such as the anti-tank guided missile – as imperilling the high-speed combined arms mechanized offensive around which their army is built. Long-range artillery is needed to strike simultaneously throughout the depths of the enemy defence if the Soviet armoured spearheads are not to be defeated by ATGM-armed enemy forces. Reserve positions must be disrupted. NATO artillery, whose responsive fire missions and accurate target acquisition the Soviets still cannot match, must be counterbalanced by weight of numbers and range of fire. This is why the 34th is a key element in the Soviet combined arms forces in Germany and would be a key element in any future conflict in Europe.

This is also consistent with the discovery – apparent since Exercise Zapad-81 – that the Soviets are placing renewed emphasis on the use of Operational Manoeuvre Groups. These are mechanized forces, built around tank or motorized rifle regi-

Above: For striking beyond the reach of long-range artillery the Soviets have increasing numbers of sophisticated fighter-bombers such as this MiG-27 *Flogger-D*. The Soviets view the delivery of conventional firepower to be basically the same, whether carried out by artillery, aircraft, or surface-to-surface missiles. (US Navy)

Below: Surface-to-surface missiles join with the 34th to give the Soviet Army its long battlefield reach. This SS-21 SSM launch vehicle can carry missiles with nuclear, chemical, high-explosive or sub-munition warheads. (US Department of Defense)

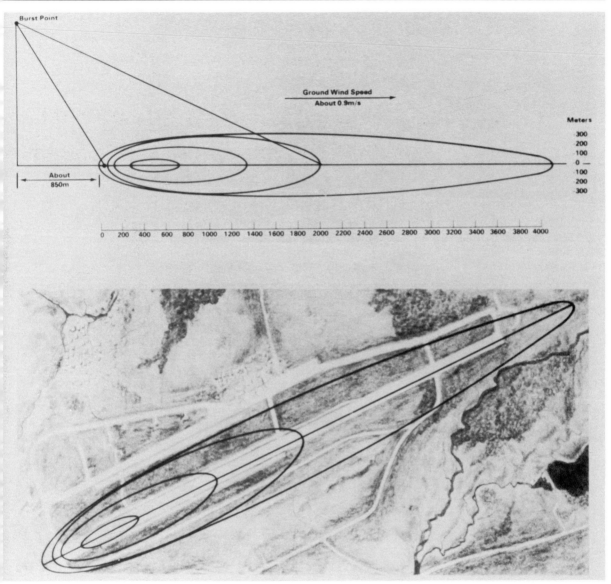

Above right: This shows the lethal 'footprint' of a single SCUD surface-to-surface chemical missile with an airburst over a NATO airfield, the 'footprint' moving progressively downwind. (US Department of Defense)

ments or, for significant objectives, divisions. They are, under current Soviet operational concepts, intended to penetrate, in mobile combat, NATO's defences – to a distance defined, in Soviet military thought, as the operational depths. To reach similar objectives, the Soviets have also organized the *Front*-level Air Assault and Airmobile Brigades which can use either parachute or helicopter vertically to penetrate the front lines.

The 34th received its new long-range artillery at about the same time as the OMG and the Air Assault Brigades achieved new importance. The 34th's heavy artillery provides the tactical long

reach in the Soviet deep battle, just as the OMG provides the operational long reach. Having longer-ranged supporting weapons in non-divisional artillery units reduces the need for artillery support which the OMGs and Air Assault Brigades will have to take with them in their penetration. Heavy guns at the base of a Soviet penetration can provide artillery support to make easier the task of keeping the OMGs moving.

Targets within 30 kilometres of the front lines can be engaged with these heavy artillery weapons or by Hind assault helicopters. There is no need for the Soviet Air Force to be pressed into the type of close air support that is not the most effective use of high-performance jet aircraft.

The 34th is equipped with digital computers in its fire control system. While not as advanced as Western systems, they are still a great advance over the Second World War-vintage systems which were used into the 1970s. Command Observation Posts now have a computer system on a tracked vehicle with them. There are more target acquisition means available to Soviet commanders. Laser rangefinders are in widespread use, with a maximum range of twenty kilometres and a practical range of ten kilometres. Hind helicopters may also provide targeting for Soviet heavy artillery striking at targets deep in NATO positions.

New munitions exist for new missions. The urbanized terrain of northern Europe provides a number of potential choke-points and backstops for Soviet forces attempting to penetrate the operational depths of NATO. While the Soviet forces would try to bypass such defended areas whenever possible, there would be times when they would have to be attacked. This is where the incendiary submunition comes in, delivered from 122mm rockets, BM-27s, or from aircraft-dropped canisters. These weapons give the Soviets a tremendous capability, especially in urban fighting, to literally incinerate whole areas with battery or battalion volleys of rockets, and reduce the need for the Soviets to take such areas by slow and costly house-to-house fighting. Also for use in urban fighting, the Soviet M1976 240mm self-propelled mortar has not only HE and chemical and nuclear rounds, but a newly developed Concrete Piercing round. This new shell gives the 240mm mortar great urban combat capability, as such rounds would penetrate even the strongest buildings.

Other munitions which these new heavy artillery weapons can fire include Artillery Fired Atomic Projectiles (AFAPs). The Soviets are obviously trying to replace as many non nuclear-capable artillery weapons with nuclear-capable ones. While the Soviets themselves have always avoided identifying any particular one of

their weapons as being nuclear-capable, Western sources believe that the new 152mm field gun (towed and self-propelled) and self-propelled howitzer, 240mm mortar, and 203mm gun are all dual-capable. The 34th is not seen primarily as a nuclear-delivery unit, this being the mission of the High Command Reserve High Power Artillery Brigades, independent brigades which report directly to the Supreme High Command (*Stavka*) in Moscow.

HEAVY ARTILLERY AND THE BATTLE IN CENTRAL EUROPE

The USA and its NATO allies have been looking to increase the forward reach of their tactical and operational forces through the development of concepts such as AirLand Battle, Deep Strike, and Emerging Technologies. While these programmes have been getting under way, the Soviets have been aiming to achieve a similar capability, but by different means.

The strength of Soviet artillery means that any force put into the front line against the Soviets in Central Europe will either have to be mechanized – personnel in armoured vehicles are largely protected from casualties by fragments – or well entrenched in field fortifications or built-up areas. Otherwise, they run the risk of suffering prohibitive losses from Soviet artillery. This means that cheap, light forces are unlikely to provide an effective defence for Europe, even if they are using state-of-the-art technology.

The effectiveness of Soviet artillery on a future European battlefield depends on how wide the gap turns out to be between the capability the Soviets have on paper and their actual performance. Peacetime standards have historically been poor predictors of actual performance; it being said that no combat-ready unit ever passed inspection and no inspection-ready unit ever passed combat. While, in Twentieth Century warfare, quality has often defeated quantity, the Soviets have enough strength inherent in their overall way of war – the whole is stronger than the parts – that it should be able to compensate for the equally inherent weaknesses. Artillery is

Left: The 2S4 M-1975 SP 240mm mortar is part of the process of improvemet of Soviet long-range artillery that included the BM-27. It currently serves alongside BM-27-equipped brigades in the heavy artillery of Group Soviet Forces Germany. (US Department of Defense)

one area where mass can be used to compensate for limitations. One reason why Soviet combat units are often supported by three times as many tubes as their NATO counterparts is because they lack the ability to rapidly shift control of fires that NATO relies on.

Soviet numerical superiority requires concentration, of firepower as well as men and units, at the decisive point. During the Second World War, the Soviets seldom had overwhelming numerical superiority when the two sides were compared overall on the Eastern Front. When the Soviets went over to the offensive, they would mass forces to achieve great numerical superiority at the decisive points, where the breakthrough and penetration were to take place. The lethality of modern weapons, conventional as well as nuclear, along with the faster tempo of modern warfare (in which all combat units are mechanized and all support units are motorized, unlike the Eastern Front) means that the concentration and build-up of troops will now have to be replaced in part, by concentration of firepower. Today, Soviet long-range artillery fire can be concentrated on the decisive point while the weapons themselves are dispersed over a large area. The increase in the number of Soviet artillery pieces high-readiness battalions have been increased from 18 to 24 – as well as the shift from towed to self-propelled weapons have been intended to increase concentration and mobility of firepower.

All of this puts a premium on logistics. The success of the Soviet conventional offensive, with its fast movement, far-ranging OMGs, and intense 'fire strikes' depends on the ability of the Soviet logistics system to provide supplies. It is uncertain whether it can do so. The Soviet emphasis on a short war and a quick victory is intended to reduce the importance of logistics. The Soviets have also devoted much time and effort to improving their logistical system, which is today much more capable than the one which failed so spectacularly in the 1968 invasion of Czechoslovakia. But Soviet logistic performance in Afghanistan has often been marginal, despite the short distance and the absence of enemy airstrikes. This certainly raises questions about its effectiveness in a potential war in Europe.

The RPG-16, currently standard man-carried anti-tank weapon in 6th Guards Airborne Division.

4

6TH GUARDS AIRBORNE DIVISION, BELOGORSK, FAR EASTERN MILITARY DISTRICT, USSR

THE garrisons of Siberia and the Soviet Far East are concrete growths on the route of the Trans-Siberian Railway. There, the military impetus of Russia's drive eastward is obvious, starting with the Tsarist frontier posts. The East has always been full of enemies – the Mongols in the thirteenth century, the Japanese and Chinese in the twentieth – as well as riches, gold and ivory then, oil and gas now. Both have necessitated a strong military presence.

The 6th Guards Airborne Division is part of that presence – garrisoned at Belogorsk, in the Far Eastern Military District, poised for action against China, Korea, or Japan, or even farther afield.

■ THE SOVIET ARMY IN ASIA

In the Soviet Union's long and difficult relationship with China, the army has been both shield and sword. China claims much of the border area, including some of the path of the Trans-Siberian Railway. In the most heated years of the Cultural Revolution, the Chinese threat may have looked very real indeed to Moscow. Not only does Russia's loathing of her Asian neighbours date back to the Mongols, but the competition in ideology and geopolitics made much of the 1960s and 1970s a tense time in Belogorsk and the other garrisons.

Today, China apparently has neither the capability nor the intention of crossing the

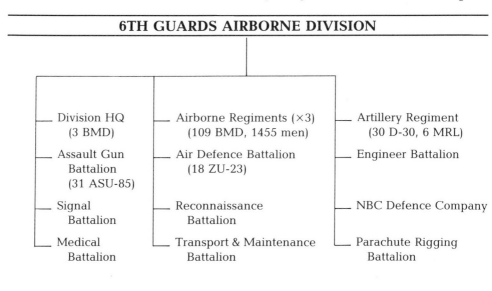

6TH GUARDS AIRBORNE DIVISION

- Division HQ (3 BMD)
- Assault Gun Battalion (31 ASU-85)
- Signal Battalion
- Medical Battalion
- Airborne Regiments (×3) (109 BMD, 1455 men)
- Air Defence Battalion (18 ZU-23)
- Reconnaissance Battalion
- Transport & Maintenance Battalion
- Artillery Regiment (30 D-30, 6 MRL)
- Engineer Battalion
- NBC Defence Company
- Parachute Rigging Battalion

Siberian border. The messianic outreach of Mao has gone to the junkheap of history. The only wars of national liberation Communist China is actively supporting are those in Afghanistan, Cambodia, Laos, Vietnam; fighting Soviet-backed Communist regimes. China has not shown any intention of directly confronting the Soviet Union. Military modernization has only fourth place in the 'five moderns' programme, and the size of the active component of the People's Liberation Army has been reduced by one million.

The Soviets, however, have not reacted to the changes in China by reducing their forces in Asia. Rather, have they increased them. The Soviets realize that Asia and the Pacific are going to be the areas of conflict and growth into the twenty-first century. The Soviet Union's growing Pacific reach is evident in its overtures to the island-states of the South Pacific and, more concretely, to its relation with Vietnam. The Soviets have expanded the base at Cam Ranh Bay – one of the world's great natural harbours

– which provides a staging-point not only for the Soviet Navy and its lean, grey Backfire bombers, but for the 6th Guards Airborne Division as well, should the Kremlin require its presence that far from its Siberian home.

At one time 'sent to Khamchatka' described any Soviet officer in a dead-end career, such as counting paper clips in the Ministry of Defence. Today, however, the Far East is far from a dead end. Ever since the first operational peacetime theatre of operations high command (GTVD) was set up in the Far East in the late 1970s and early 1980s, the Far East has been seen as militarily important; consequently, those who do well there have thrived throughout the army.

In the Far Eastern theatre of operations, as throughout the Soviet Army, the basic posture is offensive. Against China, the 6th Airborne would certainly be part of any future conflict. The key limitation to the Soviet ability to make war on China is logistics. All supplies would have to move

Above: If the 6th Guards Airborne Division had to deploy over long distances, it would probably be in Il-76 Candid transports such as this one, of both the Air Force and Aeroflot. (US Navy)

over the Trans-Siberian or the parallel, but more northerly, Baikal-Amur Mainline (BAM). Once the supplies were in-theatre, it would take a tremendous effort to re-supply a Soviet invasion force. To move at the rates of advance that the Soviets postulate in a conventional war – 35 kilometres a day – an astronomical amount of fuel would be consumed as well as ammunition. Following the widespread logistics failures which occurred during the 1968 invasion of Czechoslovakia, the Soviets have moved to modernize their logistics system. Whether it could cope with the vast distances and huge consumption of a war in Asia is uncertain.

THE AIRBORNE AND ANTI-TANK WARFARE

Anti-tank weapons are especially important to airborne forces. During the Second World War the Soviets saw how German armoured reserves, few in number, were able to mop up any of their paratroops who tried to stand against them. Arnhem must have also served notice that courage and light weapons alone will not let paratroops prevail over armour. The answer has been to equip Soviet airborne divisions with BMDs and RPGs as their tank-killing systems.

The BMD is the lighter airborne version of the BMP. The 6th Guards Airborne Division, like all Soviet airborne divisions, has enough BMDs for all its rifle battalions. This gives it a capability for mechanized movement and self-propelled tank-killing. The 6th is trained to fight with or without its BMDs. It would take them if the Soviets were able to concentrate large numbers of transport aircraft, as by combining the assets of the Air Force and Aeroflot, the state airline, the Soviets can simultaneously lift three divisions at short range. If the 6th were to deploy into another theatre, it would probably leave its BMDs, to be brought in by a follow-up echelon as airlift permitted. This makes the RPG series of

hand-held anti-tank weapons more valuable to the Soviet airborne, than to the rest of the Army.

Throughout the Second World War, while the Soviets could count on increasingly effective and numerous tanks and anti-tank guns, the infantry still had to defend itself from tanks by using hand-grenades, anti-tank rifles, and improvised munitions. Thus, in 1944–45, when advancing Soviet forces captured large numbers of German Panzerfausts, they were quickly pressed into service. First introduced by the Germans in 1943, the Panzerfaust is a single-shot, disposable recoilless, anti-tank grenade-launcher which destroyed many Soviet tanks during the last two years of the war. Impressed by the new weapon, the Soviets shipped an entire Panzerfaust factory from the Soviet zone of occupied German to Russia. Soon they were being produced as the RPG-1 (RPG = *Reaktivniy Protivotankovyi Granatomet*, rocket-powered anti-tank grenade-launcher).

Larger, reloadable versions of this Soviet weapon were developed: first, the RPG-2 and, in the 1960s, the RPG-7. One RPG-7 was issued to each motorized rifle squad. Its gunner was also armed with a Kalashnikov assault rifle and was assisted by a loader, who carried both the ammunition for the RPG and his own Kalashnikov.

Soviet motorized rifle units are mechanized, combined arms units. The Soviet Army has no 'leg' infantry divisions. Each squad has its own BTR-60/70/80 series

6TH GUARDS AIRBORNE DIVISION

MEN	6,500
BMD (including 60 without turrets)	330
D-30 122mm Howitzer	30
M-1975 122mm multiple rocket-launcher	6
120mm mortar (SP or towed)	18
ASU-85 assault gun	31
SA-7 or SA-14 SAM launcher	183
ZU-23 23mm twin AA gun	36
BRDM-2 SP ATGM launcher	27
RPG-16D AT weapon	421
AGS-17 30mm grenade-launcher	54
RPK-74 5.45mm LMG	301
BRDM-2 scout car	8

wheeled armoured personnel carrier armed with a 14.5mm heavy machine-gun or BMP-1 or BMP-2 tracked infantry combat vehicle, armed with a 73mm or 30mm cannon and a Sagger, Spigot, or Spandrel anti-tank guided missile-launcher. The squad consists of nine to eleven men, heavily armed with one or two 5.45mm or 7.62mm machine-guns, the RPG-7 gunner, and five to seven riflemen with Kalshnikovs – quite a powerful command for a junior sergeant with as little as six months' service.

The same applies to the airborne tactical subunits of the 6th and the other Soviet airborne divisions. Each squad has its own BMD. In addition to the two-man BMD crew of gunner and driver, there is the sergeant squad leader, who commands the

Above: The standard Soviet tactical transport remains the An-12 Cub, which is similar to the West's C-130 Hercules. If Soviet paratroops had to drop into combat, they would probably do so in An-12s. It has also been used as a bomber in Afghanistan, the bombs being rolled down the rear ramp.

AIRBORNE BMD SQUAD

Assault Line

Machine-gun loader
AKD & RPG-18

6–8m

Machine-gunner
5.45mm RPKS-74

BMD to rear

Squad leader
AKD & RPG-18

RPG gunner
RPG-16 & AKD

50–60m

RPG loader
AKD & RPG ammo

Driver AKSU

Gunner AKD

c. 50m

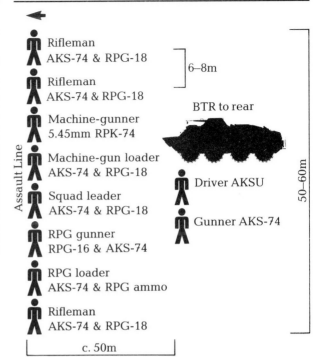

MOTORIZED RIFLE BTR SQUAD

Assault Line

Rifleman
AKS-74 & RPG-18

6–8m

Rifleman
AKS-74 & RPG-18

Machine-gunner
5.45mm RPK-74

BTR to rear

Machine-gun loader
AKS-74 & RPG-18

Squad leader
AKS-74 & RPG-18

Driver AKSU

RPG gunner
RPG-16 & AKS-74

Gunner AKS-74

50–60m

RPG loader
AKS-74 & RPG ammo

Rifleman
AKS-74 & RPG-18

c. 50m

Right: A BMD-1 on the
ground while others
descend by triple-canopy
parachutes. (US Army)

Above left: A BMD-1 airborne infantry fighting vehicle. Armed with a 73mm cannon and an anti-tank guided missile (either a modified Sagger, as here, or a more modern Spigot), the BMDs provide much of the 6th Guards Airborne's anti-tank capability. (US Army)

Left: Paratroopers deploying a 120mm M-1943 heavy mortar. Each of the 6th Guards Airborne Division's airborne battalions has a battery of these weapons. Paratroopers of any nation rely heavily on their mortars for indirect fire support.

Above right: Squads of paratroopers in squad skirmish lines with RPGs and light machine-guns in the middle around the squad leader follow ASU-85s into the attack. The 6th Guards Airborne Division has 31 ASU-85s. Although obsolescent, they are the heaviest armour available to the division. (US Navy)

Right: A 122mm BM-21 MRL ready to fire. The crew will retire to foxholes or a suitable position to avoid the rocket blasts on firing.

squad mounted or on foot. Riding in the rear of the BMD, or dismounting to fight on foot, are a 5.45mm RPK-74 light machine-gunner, two riflemen, and a gunner for the squad's RPG-7D or RPG-16D.

THE RPG-7

The RPG-7 is, together with its successor, the RPG-16, the main weapon of the Soviet airborne soldier against enemy tanks. Before firing an RPG-7, the gunner or loader assembles a round, either the PG-7 or PG-7M HEAT (High-Explosive Anti-Tank, the standard round) or OG-7 High Explosive, screwing the warhead and sustainer motor to the booster charge. The assembled round is then loaded into the muzzle of the RPG launcher.

The optical sight on the RPG-7 is a relatively complex piece of equipment. To determine the range to the target, a stadia is marked on the sight. The gunner puts the baseline on the tank's treads. The mark the turret top touches shows the range in hundreds of metres. This system does not work if the tank is more or less than 2.7 metres high or if it is in a hull-down position, with only the turret exposed. Then, the gunner must use a memorized formula or, more likely, a good guess.

Having found the range, the RPG gunner must then elevate his weapon, with range lines marked on his sight at 100-metre intervals from 200 to 500 metres. The difficult part is leading a moving target, especially in a cross-wind. The fin-stabilized, rocket-propelled RPG-7 round has a tendency to turn into the wind, and the

Above left: The 6th Guards Airborne Division's main air defence weapons are hand-held SA-7 or SA-14 SAM launchers and twin-barrelled ZU-23 23mm anti-aircraft guns, such as this one, being fired by paratroopers.

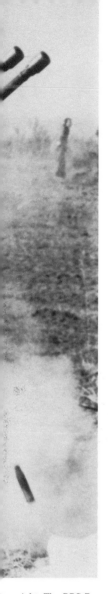

ove right: The RPG-7
1own here) or RPG-16
1nner is the heart of
:h Soviet motorized
e or airborne squad's
ability against
noured vehicles.

gunner must calculate that as well.

This is a fairly intricate procedure. The optimum range for RPG is 300 metres: rather close if an angry tank has just been missed. A simpler solution is to use the tangent sights on the front of the weapon which have elevation lines but lack the elaborate rangefinding and deflection lines.

Pulling the trigger ignites a powder charge which fires the grenade from the tube, four stabilizing fins popping open as the round is ejected. The warhead arms after the grenade has travelled five metres and, after eleven metres the sustainer rocket ignites, boosting the grenade to a maximum velocity of 294 metres per second. If it does not hit anything in five seconds, the round self-destructs. The RPG-7 can punch a 2-inch hole through 280mm of armour plate.

In the hands of determined troops –even if unskilled – RPG-7s can inflict considerable casualties on armoured forces. The world-wide employment of the RPG-7 is one reason why there are few low-technology threats left in the world today. Just about every army or guerrilla force has substantial numbers of RPG-7s or its Western counterparts. RPG-7s cannot stop an armoured thrust by themselves – their limitations are apparent from the drill required to load, aim, and fire – but they can inflict painful losses. In the 1973 Middle East War, the weapon that destroyed the most Israeli tanks on the northern front was the RPG-7. In Vietnam, RPGs were the second biggest killer of Allied armour, after mines. In Afghanistan the Soviets have lost many tanks to

RPG-7s. Throughout the world, terrorist groups – including the Provisional IRA – have found the RPG-7 a cheap and useful addition to their fire-power.

NATO tanks would have to operate as part of a combined arms team, with infantry, mechanized or on foot, to suppress and destroy the RPG gunners. Tanks must move, when possible, from cover to cover. Close cooperation with artillery will also help remove the RPG-7 threat. Tank armour can help reduce the effectiveness of an RPG round even if it hits. Modern, composite tank armour, such as that on the M1 Abrams or the Challenger, will also turn the RPG-7 into a rather mediocre tank killer. Other, older vehicles can gain protection by the use of Vietnam-era 'RPG screens' portable wire mesh which can be put around a stationary vehicle or used as appliqué armour on a moving one; they will short out the piezo-electric fuzes of 50 per cent of all RPG rounds.

THE RPG-16

The standard squad-level anti-tank weapon in the 6th Guards Airborne Division is the two-part RPG-16D paratroop model of the RPG-16, which has replaced the similar paratroop model of the RPG-7, the RPG-7D. This is consistent with overall Soviet Army practise, for the RPG-16 has been the replacement to the RPG-7 as the Soviet Army's squad-level man-carried anti-tank rocket-launcher since the late 1970s.

The RPG-16 round, like that of the RPG-7, is a rocket-propelled grenade with a shaped-charge High Explosive Anti-Tank (HEAT) warhead. Although, externally, the RPG-16 launcher resembles the RPG-7, the round is quite different. It is shorter – 600cm long as opposed to the 905cm-long RPG-7 round with its extended 'tail' which the RPG-16 round lacks. The RPG-16 round is of a smaller calibre but gives better performance. It is a modernized design and is considerably more accurate and easier to use than the RPG-7, which cannot be comforting to those whose normal place of business is in an APC. The RPG-16 round is faster, which means it is less liable to be affected by cross-winds than the RPG-7 round. The fin design on the RPG-16 round also appears better, as more stability is provided by its higher muzzle velocity. Because the round will arrive quicker and less affected by cross-winds, aiming the RPG-16 will be easier than aiming the RPG-7. This has led to a significant increase in effective range over the RPG-7 – from 300–500 metres to 500–800 metres.

The Afghans have captured a few RPG-16s, but they have seen only limited use. Some prefer the earlier RPG-7 despite its inferior performance because they have had experience with it and their gunners have finally succeeded in mastering the weapon's intricacies. Because resupply is difficult, the Afghans have tried to standardize on a few items of equipment, and one-off RPG-16s may be sold to buy more of the less effective but more widely known RPG-7s.

THE RPG-18

Each of the rifle squads of the 6th Guards Airborne Division will probably carry two or three RPG-18s, the Soviet Light Anti-tank Weapon (LAW). In the British and US Armies, LAWs are given out to individual men, like rounds of ammunition. While new weapons are replacing them – the British LAW-80 or the US AT-4 – the current issue British and US LAW is the 66mm M72. Not coincidentally, the Soviet LAW, the RPG-18, is a copy of the same weapon, and is distributed in the same way to Soviet troops. This use of Western designs and technology is standard Soviet practice when they need a weapons system that has been developed abroad and there is no Soviet equivalent.

After the use of captured Panzerfausts – the original LAW – in 1944–45, the Soviet relied on shaped-charge anti-tank hand-grenades as their LAW for many years. These were large and heavy, with drogue parachutes in their handle to make sure they landed at the correct angle of impact on top on a tank. This meant they had to be dropped from a window or lofted with a close-range underhand throw. The latest version of these grenades, the RKG-3M, is still used in action by Kabul Regime troops in Afghanistan – possibly because the Soviets took away all their ally's RPG-7s in

Right: The best known RPG, the standard RPG-7.

ANTI-TANK WEAPONS

	RPG-7	RPG-16	RPG-18
Launcher			
Tube calibre (mm)	40	58.3	64
Length (m)	0.953	1.1	1.05 (extended) 0.705 (closed)
Weight (kg)	7.9 (empty)	10.3	2.7 (grenade & launcher
Type			
Warhead calibre (mm)	85	58.3	64
Length (m)	0.905	0.6	0.67
Weight, complete round (kg)	2.25	3.0	1.4
Performance			
Muzzle velocity (m/s)	120	130	115
Maximum velocity (m/s)	300	350	300
Effective range (m)	300–500	500–800	200
Armour penetration (mm @ 0° obliquity @ any range)	330	up to 375	up to 375
Rate of fire (rpm)	4–6	4–6	one shot
Crew	1	1	1
Introduced	1962	late 1970s	late 1970s

the 1980s when they were ending up in the hands of the guerrillas. Soviets returned to the basic Panzerfaust approach, when, in the 1970s, they deployed the RPG-18.

The Soviets are as well aware of the limitations of the M72, as British and US troops have been aware for years. It has limited effectiveness against tanks such as the US M1 Abrams or the British Challenger, or even, it appears, tanks with Israeli Blazer active armour.

The RPG-18 is a proven design, and it is inexpensive and easy to produce. The RPG-18's rocket is slightly longer and heavier than that of the US M72, with a new shaped-charge warhead providing greater penetration than would be expected from a weapon of 63.5mm calibre. The RPG-18 is thus more likely to kill the tanks it hits than the M72. Once the tube has been extended into firing position from its collapsed carrying position, the tube cover folded down and the sights snapped up, the RPG-18 (unlike the M72) must be fired – it cannot be disarmed.

Like the M72, the RPG-18 is a throw-away weapon, although, in peacetime, the

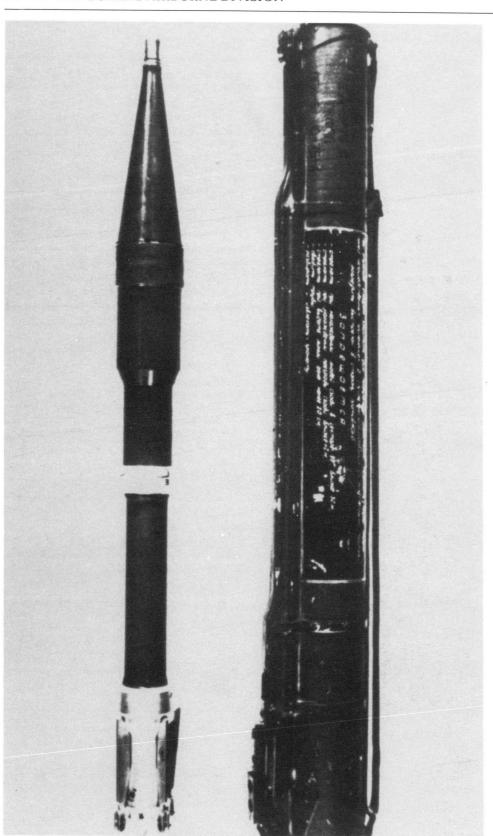

Left: An RPG-18, the Soviet soldier's standard personal anti-tank weapon.

Right: An RPG-16 captured by the Afghan Resistance. (US Information Agency)

empty tube is retained for recycling. The Soviets have also copied the M72's sub-calibre firing device for training purposes. A large decal in Cyrillic is applied to the outer tube of each RPG-18, which the Soviets believe should give even untrained troops a good idea of how to use the weapon. Its compact size and protective plastic covering makes the RPG-18 easy to carry.

The RPG-18 is issued, in crates of eight rounds, as ammunition. Each Soviet motor-ized rifle or airborne squad would carry, on the average, two or three RPG-18s, but would stock up if heavy armoured opposi-tion was expected or if they were operating dismounted without tanks or BMDs to provide supporting fire-power. Each Soviet squad retains its RPG-7 or RPG-16 anti-tank rocket-launcher.

The Soviets have made extensive use of the RPG-18 in Afghanistan. As US troops in Vietnam and British troops in the Falk-lands used the M72 to destroy bunkers, houses and fortified positions, the Soviets have discovered that an RPG-18 round will remove a *sangar* (an Afghan rock breast-work) and anyone behind it, where a burst of small-arms ammunition would only splatter against the rocks.

To fire the RPG-18, the soldier extends the tube like a telescope, then unfolds the trigger and safety catch, rear peep sights,

folding front sight (with range calibrations at 50-metre intervals up to 200 metres) and removes the front and rear tube covers. The weapon must then be armed and can be fired prone, kneeling or standing, pro-vided that the backblast area is clear. The piezo-electric nose fuze of the rocket is armed at two to fifteen metres' range. If the fuze is not activated after four to six seconds flight time, it will self-destruct.

The RPG-18 is probably only an interim measure, until the Soviets can field a more advanced design against modern tanks. An improved version, reportedly desig-nated RPG-22, was in action in Afghani-stan in 1987. It also shows that the Soviets are not technologically backward. Even if it means the adoption of foreign designs, they can give their troops weapons as good as those of their opponents – while retain-ing the traditional numerical advantage.

RPG TACTICS

In a motorized rifle or airborne squad, the RPG-7 or RPG-16 is normally positioned, in attack or defence, next to the squad leader, so that he can direct its fire. Because of the limited effective range of the RPG – es-pecially when compared to a tank's arma-ment – camouflage, concealment and surprise are need to get close to a tank. The Soviets use 'fire pockets' and anti-tank ambushes to assure a killing shot. When-ever possible, the RPGs are integrated with other weapons into a larger, overall scheme of anti-tank defence. Thus, a tank turning to avoid a minefield would turn its flanks to concealed RPGs.

Anti-tank ambushes can also be used as an offensive tactic. Creeping up on armoured units in night positions and using RPG-7s with the NSP-2 night sight has been one way for guerrillas to inflict casualties on mechanized enemy forces. The North Vietnamese and the Afghan guerrillas have both used RPG-7s effec-tively in this way.

The introduction of the OG-7 high-explosive round in the 1970s now allows each Soviet motorized rifle and airborne squad to put down fire with the punch of a light mortar and the accuracy of a direct fire weapon. RPGs have frequently been used against helicopters in Rhodesia,

Vietnam and now, in Afghanistan. While aiming at a moving helicopter is difficult, hovering helicopters are vulnerable.

AT THE OTHER END OF ASIA: AIRBORNE IN AFGHANISTAN

While the 6th itself has its area of operations further east, the Soviet Airborne Forces have been closely linked with the war in Afghanistan since December 1979. The opening stages of the war showed how the 6th and divisions like it would act in a future conflict, for the invasion itself underlined the operational-level mission of the airborne and how it can be effectively performed. In Kabul in 1979, as in Prague in 1968, the Soviet airborne flew in, linked up with *Spetsnaz* and agents in place, and was able to pre-empt organized resistance by seizing key targets such as communications centres, headquarters, airfields, and road choke-points. This is what the 6th would try and do if committed to battle elsewhere in Asia.

Afghanistan in 1979 also saw the commitment of airborne forces from throughout the Soviet Union, an indication of what could be expected elsewhere. Not only was the whole of the 105th Guards Airborne Division deployed, but so were regiments from the 103rd Guards Airborne – the Soviet Army's airborne 'fire brigade' for rapid deployment – and the 104th Guards Airborne.

In 1980, the Soviets took the unusual step of disbanding one of their eight Guards Airborne Divisions – the 105th. The 103rd permanently moved its headquarters to Afghanistan, where it remains today.

Since 1979, the Soviet Airborne Forces in Afghanistan have been deployed on missions which have kept at least some units around Kabul literally as a 'palace guard' for the Soviet viceregal court and possibly as a power-protection force for southern Asia and Persian Gulf contingencies. The commitment of paratroops to battle has not always lead to success. In the 1984 Panjsher VII offensive, no less than four airborne regiments were used, and they did not achieve much greater success than the previous offensives using mainly

motorized rifle troops. In this offensive, as in Panjsher V, two years before, a battalion-sized helicopter-inserted force, presumably of paratroops, was badly cut up by the Afghans. But the paratroops remain an excellent source for special operations forces. They have fit, pre-trained, troops. The motivation and aggressiveness that comes with airborne status is one reason why armies throughout the world tend to have more paratroops than they can drop. They are good candidates for specialized infantry, that can receive specialist train-

Below: Paratroopers in Afghanistan. Soviet airborne forces were the first military elements into Kabul, linking up with special operations forces. The airborne regiments in the invasion were equipped with 73mm-armed BMD-1 airborne infantry fighting vehicles. (US Department of Defense)

ing for night, mountain, or counter-insurgency operations. While to the West the mix of airborne and mountain training may seem strange, Soviet Airborne Forces have emphasized mountain operations since before the Afghanistan war. Of eighteen airborne-related articles appearing in *Military Herald*, the Soviet Army's tactical magazine for junior and field grade officers, in the three years prior to the war, six were devoted to seizing mountain passes.

Airborne units, along with air assault brigades and battalions, *Spetsnaz*, and motorized rifle battalions trained in heliborne operations, are perhaps 20% of the Soviet forces committed to the Afghanistan war, but constitute most of the offensive capability, although they also suffer from the poor morale that plagues the Soviet forces in Afghanistan and their tactics reflect Soviet attempts to minimize the rate of casualties. While they will remain vital to Soviet tactics, the 1987 battles have shown that even these forces can be defeated on the battlefield.

What the 35th Air Assault Brigade would look like going into action: a squadron-sized formation of Mi-8 Hip-Cs looking like the Soviet remake of *Apocalypse Now*. Such formations would be supported by Hind attack helicopters. (US Navy)

5
35TH AIR ASSAULT BRIGADE, COTTBUS, EAST GERMANY

THE Stukas are long gone from Cottbus airfield. The ugly, cranked-wing, fixed-gear dive-bombers once based there became, in 1939–41, the image of the *Blitzkrieg*, of rapid German victories against opponents too slow to react politically or militarily to the brutal realities of modern war and modern life. The image has persisted long after the Stukas themselves had fallen to the Spitfires defending England or Malta.

What flies now at Cottbus is as ugly as the Stuka. Known as the Gorbach (hunchback) to its crews and the Hind to NATO, the Mil Mi-24 attack helicopter has become as much a symbol of Soviet power as the Stuka was for Germany. In Afghanistan, Nicaragua, and Angola, it is the Hind that is the most powerful weapon in Communism's arsenal. The Hind, though the Stuka of the 1980s, still has not encountered its present-day Spitfire.

The Hind is not targeted solely against Third World peoples resisting Communist governments; it would play a critical role in any future conflict in Europe. Those at Cottbus are a key element of Group Soviet Forces Germany's capability to strike deep and hard at NATO. Although part of the Air Force, the unified Soviet command structure integrates the Hinds fully into the combined arms offensive. Those at Cottbus are even more closely linked with the army, for they are operating in support of an army unit trained and equipped for heliborne operations, the 35th Air Assault Brigade, in garrison there.

THE SOVIET ARMY AND THE HELICOPTER

The Soviet Army does not have its own aviation branch, on the model of the US

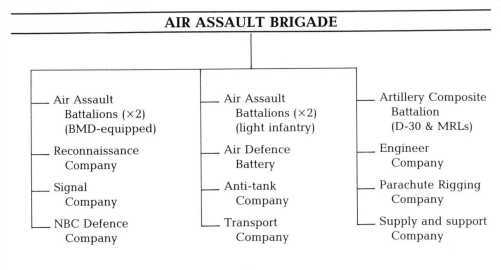

AIR ASSAULT BRIGADE

- Air Assault Battalions (×2) (BMD-equipped)
- Reconnaissance Company
- Signal Company
- NBC Defence Company

- Air Assault Battalions (×2) (light infantry)
- Air Defence Battery
- Anti-tank Company
- Transport Company

- Artillery Composite Battalion (D-30 & MRLs)
- Engineer Company
- Parachute Rigging Company
- Supply and support Company

and British Armies. All the helicopters in support of the Soviet Army are owned by the Soviet Air Force, their crews Air Force personnel. The helicopter units are, however, under the command of Army head-quarters, either at *front*, army (the level for most helicopter units, especially the regiments of attack helicopters that have been introduced into Group Soviet Forces, Germany in recent years), or division level (where high-readiness divisions have their own helicopter squadron).

The most important types of helicopter in the Soviet Air Force are the Mi-24 Hind attack helicopter and the Mi-8 and Mi-17 Hip transport helicopters. The Mi-2 Hop-lite, provides liaison and light transport capabilities, while the Mi-6 Hook is used for heavy lift missions. Some piston-engined Mi-4 Hounds, predecessor of the Hips, remain in service.

The Mi-24 Hind is the Soviet Union's 'flying tank'. The single most hated and feared weapon in the war in Afghanistan, Hinds are heavily armed, with 12.7mm machine-guns (a single barrel in the early Hind-A, a 3-barrel Gatling type in others). Their armament is mounted on two stub wings, each with two hardpoints. These hardpoints can each be used to carry 250kg bombs or canister bomblet con-

tainers, 57mm rocket pods (each containing 32 rockets with high-explosive or shaped-charge warheads), or chemical warfare canisters (Hinds have been one of the primary means of delivering poison gas in Afghanistan). At the end of the stub wings are launchers for anti-tank guided missiles – a total of four. These weapons are the primary armament of the Hind in a conventional conflict.

The Hind is built to take punishment as well as inflict it. Despite a number of weak

AIR ASSAULT BRIGADE

Men	2,000–2,60
BMD airborne infantry fighting vehicles	6
BRDM-2 scout cars	
D-30 122mm towed howitzers	1
122mm M-1975 SP multiple rocket-launchers	
120mm M-1943 mortars	2
SA-7/14/16 launchers	4
23mm ZU-23 twin AA guns	
ATGM-armed BRDM-2 scout cars	
Manpacked ATGMs	1
73mm SPG-9 recoilless anti-tank guns	3
85mm SD-44 anti-tank guns	
RPG-16D anti-tank weapons	15
30mm AGS-17 grenade-launchers	2
5.45mm RPK-74 light machine-guns	11

Left: Heavily armed, this Hip-E is much better at inflicting punishment than taking it – it lacks even the appliqué armour that is seen on some examples. It is armed with no less than six 57mm rocket pods, four ATGM racks, and a 12.7mm machine-gun or 30mm grenade-launcher in the nose. Such Hip-Es can provide powerful suppressive firepower for the 35th. The Soviet Union's East German allies use the export model, the Hip-F.

points – the main rotor hub is one – it has integral titanium belly armour and key parts of its structure are protected against .50 calibre gunfire, as are the crew.

Production of these helicopters continues at a high rate: Hind production is 150–180 machines a year. Total helicopter production for 1982 was 700 aircraft. In 1983, the Soviet Air Force's Hind strength was 1,035 and their Hip strength was 1,615. These are supplemented by the considerable Aeroflot helicopter fleet whose Hips are capable of using the same strap-on weapons pods and minelaying equipment as the Air Force versions.

The existing designs are being upgraded as well as being produced. In 1982, the Hind-F appeared. Instead of the 12.7mm turret-mounted Gatling gun of the Hind-D and -E, it has two package-mounted cannon – believed to be 23mm – on the fuselage sides, under the cockpit, mounted in a manner reminiscent of wartime B-25 Mitchell and B-26 Marauder bombers. The Hind-F is believed also to have an air-to-air radar gunsight and to be able to fire air-to-air missiles. The anti-armour Hinds have also improved their capabilities, with the Hind-E using the Spiral anti-tank guided missile. Both the Hind-E and the Hip-E are said to have active and passive

infra-red countermeasures, including a chaff-flare decoy system. This has been seen in use in Afghanistan from 1982–83, indicating that the Soviets are aware of the use of SA-7 heat-seeking SAMS by the Afghan guerrillas. From 1983 the Hind force in Afghanistan has been used to a greater extent at night, without the use of flares for illumination, but using their sophisticated sensors. In the past, they had appeared either unwilling or unable to employ them.

In September, 1986, three of a flight of four Hinds were destroyed by Afghans using US-made Stinger SAMs. Throughout 1987, the powerful Soviet helicopter force found it difficult to adapt to the new weapons. Flares, infrared jammers, and exhaust shrouding have all had limited success. By late 1987, the Soviets had greatly reduced helicopter operations in Afghanistan. Helicopters fly at night or extremely low altitude, under effective Stinger altitude. Resupply missions have been curtailed, leading to the evacuation of some posts. Attack and transport missions are also limited, greatly reducing firepower and tactical mobility. Losses have reached the high point of the war.

The Mi-26 Halo, the new Soviet heavy lift helicopter, has been committed to

Right: Soviet troopers move out from a Hip-C. In Afghanistan the helicopter would still be hovering, the troopers would be wearing body armour, and everyone would be moving much faster. (US Navy)

Above: A Soviet Mi-6 Hook-B heavy-lift helicopter. Hooks lift for BMDs and logistics is vital if the 35th is to use its full capability in action. (US Navy)

Left: The Hips supporting the 35th can be reinforced by those used by Aeroflot, the Soviet state airline. Aeroflot aircraft were extensively used in the invasion of Afghanistan: some Aeroflot Mi-8s were seen with minelaying equipment

Afghanistan, where its lift/carrying capabilities will allow the Soviets to make greater use of air resupply rather than road convoys to reach outposts. A British journalist first saw one of these large helicopters in Aeroflot markings near Jalalabad in 1983. Another journalist saw more Halos flying between Jalalabad and Kabul in 1984.

35TH AIR ASSAULT BRIGADE LIFT REQUIREMENTS

Full brigade without BMDs	75 Hip, 35 Hook
Full brigade with BMDs	41 Hip, 125 Hook
Rifle battalion	13 Hip
Rifle battalion team	17 Hip
Battalion mortar platoon	6 Hook
BMD-equipped battalion	37 Hook
Brigade headquarters company	3 Hip
Howitzer battalion	24 Hook
Air defence battery	6 Hook
Reconnaissance company BMDs	4 Hook
Reconnaissance company no BMDs	2 Hip
Engineer company	3 Hook
Support elements	4 Hip

THE AIR-TO-AIR HELICOPTER THREAT

The Soviets have apparently decided that the best countermeasures to a helicopter is another helicopter, just as tanks are normally considered the best weapons to defeat other tanks, or submarines other submarines.

on after the invasion. (US Navy)

Right: An Mi-26 Halo heavy-lift helicopter in Aeroflot markings. The Soviets will use both Air Force and Aeroflot Halos to carry BMDs, fuel, and ammunition into the forward areas in support of the 35th. (US Department of Defense)

The Soviet concern over NATO helicopters dates to the early 1970s. The Soviets were aware of the effective US use of a few helicopters armed with TOW ATGMs in Vietnam in 1972. The threat to the Soviet's armoured forces was brought home during a series of US Army exercises in Germany. There, TOW-firing attack helicopters were used against US combined-arms mechanized forces, deployed to simulate Soviet tactical organizations. The helicopter-to-tank exchange ratio was, at one test at Grafenwoehr training area, 19–1.

This experience, combined with their own research and exercise data, alerted the Soviets to the potential US helicopters have to inflict serious damage on the fast-moving tank forces upon which the Soviet Army depends for battlefield success. More and better mobile air defence weapons were part of the answer. The

Above: An Mi-24 Hind-F with twin 23mm cannon in a package-mount on the fuselage side. While this one is armed with 57mm rocket pods and racks for AT-6 Spiral ATGMs, it is believed to be able to use air-to-air missiles as well. (US Army)

Soviet's standard self-propelled anti-aircraft gun, the ZSU-23-4, is armed with a quadruple 23mm cannon mount. It will certainly reduce to scrap metal any helicopter caught in its fire. The problem, for the ZSU, is catching the helicopter. It is intended to combat jet fighter-bombers rather than helicopters, and its Gun Dish fire control radar, though updated with digital fire-control equipment, has difficulty acquiring and tracking extremely low-flying targets, such as attack helicopters. The effective range of the 23mm – 3,000 metres – is less than that of a TOW ATGM – 3,750 metres. The ZSUs are supplemented by SA-9 SAM launchers and the man-carried SA-7s. While all these systems are in the process of being replaced – by the ZSU-30, the SA-13 and the SA-14 SAMs respectively, they are all limited to following the Soviet tanks. They cannot take the offensive against heli-

copters lurking behind a ridge or a tree-line, waiting to attack.

Jet fighters are, surprisingly, highly inefficient at catching helicopters. Not only do they frequently fail to spot helicopters at extremely low altitude, but most heat-seeking and radar-homing missiles have great difficulty picking out targets in ground return, especially if they are hovering. Only aircraft with a 'look-down, shoot-down' radar-homing missile, such as the US F-15 Eagle and the RAF's Skyflash-armed Phantoms are capable of destroying low-flying helicopters without having to go down in the weeds and chase them. Chasing a helicopter with a jet is a lot less fun than it sounds. The helicopter can hide behind trees, around hills, and dodge back and sideways. It can also hit back – a 20mm shell from an AH-1's cannon will void the warranty on most MiGs.

A helicopter, however, can not only reach out and strike enemy helicopters

HELICOPTERS

	Mi-8/ HIP-C	Mi-24/ HIND-E	Mi-26/ HALO-A
Crew	2	3	4
Troops	24	8–10	100+
Normal payload (kg)	4,000/		
(hovering takeoff)	3,000[1]	3,600	20,000
Takeoff weight (kg)	11,100	10,000	50,000
Service ceiling (m)	3,500/ 4,500[2]	2,100	4,500
Speed (km/h):			
Max. @ sea level	250	320	300
Cruising	225	310	250
Range (km):			
Max. payload	160	490	800
Max. fuel	410	540	1,200
Combat radius (km)	200	160	300+
Diameter, main rotor (m)	21.30	17.00	32.00
Length, fuselage (m)	18.30	19.00	34.00
Height, overall (m)	5.70	4.30	10.00

[1]Internal/sling. [2]Depending upon mission.

before they strike, unlike ground-based air defence, but it can also get down to nap-of-the-earth altitude and go between the trees and around hills. One of the foremost advocates of the use of air-to-air helicopters in the Soviet Air Force has been Major General Mikhail Belov. Belov appears to be the Soviet's leading 'rotor-head' and has done for helicopters what Admiral Gorshakov has done for the Navy. He is also a trenchant and interesting writer, very unlike the faceless clones that comprise most of the Soviet general officer ranks. Belov did not get his stars just for writing – he was probably commanding the helicopter forces in Afghanistan in 1979–80.

Belov's desire to use helicopters for air-to-air anti-helicopter missions has already led to a US response. The Marines are now mounting AIM-9 Sidewinder air-to-air missiles on their AH-1W attack helicopters. The US Army is providing more air-to-air training for its attack helicopter crews and considering mounting missiles as well. But the Hind is still limited in the anti-helicopter role. Its large size makes it un-manoeuvrable, especially in nap-of-the-earth flight, and it cannot compare with an AH-1 for ease in running around trees. But the air-to-air Hind-F pointed the way to the new generation of Soviet attack helicopters.

THE HAVOC

The Havoc is a new direction in Soviet helicopter design and development. It appears to be a two-seat attack helicopter, similar to the Hughes AH-64 Apache attack helicopter. This is a change from the Hind – a large, multi-purpose ship. The new Soviet helicopters may portend a change in tactics.

Attack helicopters do not have to be armoured – the German PAH-1, with its HOT anti-tank guided missiles, is not – but if the Soviets are not adopting the German-style approach of a small, light attack helicopter, it would make sense to provide armour protection, electronic counter-measures, and an engine powerful enough to lift it. That the Havoc is well armoured is apparent from its size. An integral gun is probably mounted, but the main armament

of the Havoc is likely to be its anti-tank guided missiles. It may use the same type as the Hinds. The Hind-E is known to use the AT-6 Spiral ATGM. It is mounted on helicopters in a self-contained tube. Guidance is by semi-active command line of sight (which requires the gunner to keep the target in the cross-hairs of his sight), similar to the US TOW missile as mounted on the AH-1 Cobra, the difference being that the Spiral reportedly uses radio guidance signals rather than thin wires to pass the corrections to the missile.

The Hind-F and the new Hokum are both reportedly armed with anti-helicopter weapons. This means probably an air-to-air gunsight, as on a fighter plane, and missiles.

THE HOKUM

In addition to the Havoc, the Soviets are reportedly developing a new helicopter, code-named Hokum, designed by the Kamov design bureau and weighing about six tons, which represents a change in Soviet attack helicopter development, going towards a smaller and lighter single-purpose machine. As a specialized anti-helicopter helicopter, Hokum is likely to be lighter, more manoeuvrable, and less armoured. In addition, Hokums could be used as scout helicopters to work with the attack helicopters.

The Havoc and Hokum combination will require more helicopters to be taken away from their primary anti-tank mission and used in the anti-helicopter mission, while helicopter crews will need more air-to-air training.

THE AIR ASSAULT BRIGADES AND THE SOVIET CONVENTIONAL OFFENSIVE IN EUROPE

Brigades like the 35th give the Soviet operational commander capabilities he has not had in the past. The Guards Airborne Divisions are, in peacetime, directly under the Ministry of Defence and, in wartime, at least some of them will be needed for strategic missions. Now *front*-level commanders are to have their own vertical

Above: The future of Soviet attack helicopters: the Mi-28 Havoc is the follow-on to the Hind. (US Department of Defense)

envelopment forces without having to divert units of the Guards Airborne Divisions.

The methods the air assault can use for vertical envelopment can vary. The 35th Air Assault Brigade, while intended to operate with helicopters providing either mobility, or supporting fire-power, or both, does not 'own' its helicopters. Rather, it requires the allocation of helicopters or fixed wing transport assets – the Brigade can also jump by parachute – for air mobility. The personnel in these brigades are reportedly all part of the VDV (*Vozdushno-Desantnyye Voyska*, The Soviet Airborne Forces) and are all jump-trained and wear the characteristic blue beret and striped undershirt of the Airborne Forces. The increase in capability and numbers of the Soviet helicopter force is linked to the appearance of these brigades. The need to helilift more heavy equipment, especially BMD airborne in-

fantry combat vehicles, may have led to the development of the Mi-26 Halo heavy lift helicopter. The ability of Soviet attack helicopters to suppress defences and provide air support for helicopter-inserted forces has been demonstrated in Afghanistan. The Hind is where Soviets may look for supporting fire-power for these units.

By using some of the hundreds of helicopters deployed in East Germany or quickly deployable from the Soviet Union or elsewhere in Eastern Europe, the 35th Air Assault Brigades can give Group Soviet Forces, Germany a lengthening operational reach. Similarly, helicopters are seen as a primary source of firepower for Operational Manoeuvre Groups, and air assault brigades such as the 35th will probably be supporting the OMG's mission of striking deep into NATO defences in a number of ways.

Along with the renewed emphasis on Operational Manoeuvre Groups in Soviet

Above left: The business end of a late-model Hind, in this case a Hind-D, shows its four 57mm rocket pods, launch rails for ATGMs, and 12.7mm Gatling gun with radar and sensors under the nose. (US Department of Defense).

Above right: A Hind-D fires a Swatter ATGM. The Hind poses a substantial threat to NATO's tank forces. (US Department of Defense).

HIND ANTI-TANK TACTICS

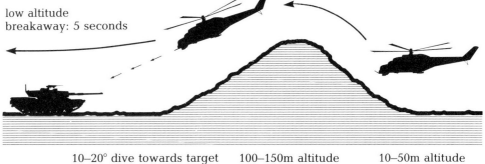

execute pop-up: 5 seconds

acquire target and fire: 3 seconds

low altitude
breakaway: 5 seconds

10–20° dive towards target   100–150m altitude   10–50m altitude

operational planning, these brigades exploit mobility and striking power. The 35th Air Assault Brigade would give a Soviet *front* commander – and in wartime, Group Soviet Forces, Germany is likely to become at least two *fronts* – capabilities to strike up to 100 kilometres deep into enemy defences. Combined with weapons such as the BM-27 220mm multiple rocket-launcher, they are another example of how the Soviet Army is evolving in the 1980s. This is part of the continued evolution in Soviet operational and tactical thinking which became apparent in the mid-1970s, with greater attention being given to 'the keys that unlock the stability of the enemy defence', such as forward detachments, airborne *desants*, and 'raiding' forces.

There are some indications of what this would mean in a future conflict. In Soviet and Warsaw Pact exercises, 'enemy' command posts, nuclear delivery means, and communication links have been targets of such air-inserted attacks. Similarly, the help of helicopter- and parachute-inserted forces to secure river crossings have been a feature of Soviet large-scale exercises since the 1960s. Follow-up echelons have been inserted by AN-12 Cubs – the Soviets seem willing to use their tactical transports in a manner similar to the way the Luftwaffe used their Ju-52s from 1939 to 1941, even if this resulted in higher aircraft losses. The BMD-equipped battalions of the air assault battalions could be air-landed – either by transports or helicopters – into positions seized by the other battalions inserted by helicopter or by parachute.

Supplementing the Air Assault Brigades such as the 35th are independent Air Assault Battalions. Each of Group Soviet Forces, Germany's four armies is believed to have one or more of these battalions. Made up of airborne-qualified personnel, but without their own helicopters, these

Top left: A two-ship element of Mi-24 Hind-Ds supports a Soviet river crossing. Helicopter-lifted Soviet units are especially valuable in river crossings, helping to seize bridgeheads.

Below left: The sting of the Hind-E, a Spiral AT-6 ATGM in its launch tube. (US Army)

battalions may carry out operations up to thirty kilometres behind the enemy front line. Organized in the 1970s and early 1980s, these battalions give a tactical air assault capability for the type of missions that previously would have required the detachment of a motorized rifle battalion from one of the army's divisions.

While there are none deployed in East Germany, elsewhere the Soviet Army has three or four airmobile brigades which have an even closer integration of troops and helicopters than even the 35th. The airmobile brigades were first organized in the early 1970s, and for the first time, substantial Frontal Aviation helicopters were placed under command of a Soviet brigade headquarters.

Until these units were organized, the Soviet Army had followed the model of the US Marine Corps who rely on using line units for helicopter lifted operations, rather than the US Army's practice of having specialized airmobile and air assault divisions.

Airmobile brigades lack large numbers of vehicles – their armoured fighting vehicle strength is limited to thirteen BRDM scout cars, nine of them armed with anti-tank guided missiles – and their organic helicopter strength is a composite regiment of 32 Mi-8 Hip medium helicopters and 24 Mi-6 Hook heavy lift helicopters. Deployed away from NATO, they may be intended to be used in battles against less intense air defences and with less need of tracked combat vehicles for the troops than would be the case in western Europe.

OTHER BATTLES, OTHER BRIGADES

The central battle in Germany is certainly not the only place where brigades such as

Below right: Mi-24 Hind-Ds with their crews. The size of the Hind – larger than either US or European attack helicopters – is readily apparent. (US Army)

the 35th would be committed. Both air assault and airmobile brigades could be involved in potential Soviet invasions of Pakistan or Iran. In Pakistan, the vital mountain passes and river crossing-places, as well as the airfields and ports, would be obvious targets.

Air assault and airmobile brigades would be invaluable to the Soviets in an invasion of Iran. The lessons of Prague in 1968 and Kabul in 1979 show the emphasis the Soviets put on the use of air-inserted forces to seize key objectives ahead of the arrival of motorized rifle divisions. Soviet tactical writings on combat in conditions such as might be found in Iran – which have proliferated since the Afghanistan War started – stress that is better to have a company at a crucial point before the enemy can react than to have a division arriving afterwards. The air assault and airmobile brigades would give the Soviets additional capabilities to seize mountain passes, airfields, road junctions, chokepoints, command and governmental centres, and other key objectives in con-

junction with airborne forces. An invasion of Iran would possibly see at least one air assault brigade employed, probably more, for such an invasion would certainly have to stress the use of heliborne forces, again, moving in quickly while the main body of the invasion advanced overland. The port of Bandar Abbas and the routes leading to it would be prime targets for an air assault brigade.

The Air Assault Brigade in the Leningrad Military District could take part in an invasion of Norway. Any such invasion would require amphibious and heliborne operations. The overland invasion routes are limited to two axes of advance – one through northern Finland and one directly from the Soviet Union, running along the coast. Both routes traverse easily defensible terrain, and by the time any Soviet forces moving overland reached their objectives south of Narvik, Norway would be mobilized and receiving NATO reinforcements.

Soviet heliborne units could be decisive. Operationally, they would cooperate with

Right: Three Hinds provide overhead cover for a Soviet tank unit in Afghanistan – part of the wide range of missions that Hinds carry out in action. (*Jamiat I Islami Afghanistan*)

Below: While the 35th uses helicopters to get to battle and the *Hind* provides considerable supporting firepower, much of its fighting must be done on foot. Here Soviet troopers move out from a Mi-8 Hip, armed with 5.45mm infantry weapons and an RPG-16 anti-tank rocket-launcher. (US Department of Defense).

naval troops infantry, paratroops, and special forces to strike directly at objectives such as airfields, ports, and pre-positioned equipment storage. Tactically, helicopters would be required to help the advance of the overland columns, seizing any position that could otherwise be turned into a miniature Monte Cassino, and vertically enveloping defending units. The airdrop capability of the air assault brigade allows it, if transport aircraft are available, to strike deeper than their helicopter's radius of action. When NATO reinforcements move to Norway, they may find that an air assault brigade has reached its destination first.

An air assault brigade could also strike into Denmark, with the same type of objectives: strike at vital points along with other power-projection forces and then hold until relieved by the tank and motorized rifle divisions. The Soviets would have air assault brigades available for a wide range of objectives. In addition to the 35th and the Air Assault Brigade in the Leningrad Military District, reportedly trained for operations in Scandinavia, there is one in Afghanistan, one in Hungary, and six more in the USSR.

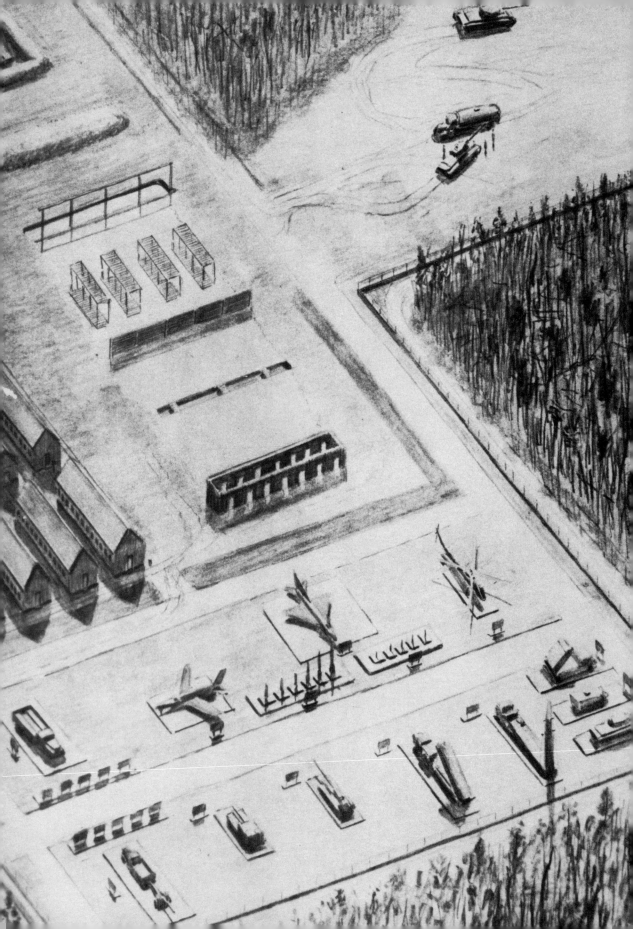

6

SPECIAL OPERATIONS BRIGADE, TRANSCAUCASUS MILITARY DISTRICT, USSR

ALL armies need a force such as that described by the French writer, Jean de Larteguy: 'Composed entirely of fit young enthusiasts in camouflage uniforms, who would not be put on display but from whom impossible efforts would be demanded and to whom all sorts of tricks would be taught. That's the army in which I should like to fight.'

This type of force exists in the Soviet Army. They do not receive much publicity, for publicity does not contribute to their mission. It is not even certain what they are called. The usual term used is *Spetsnaz*, a Russian contraction meaning special-purpose troops.

Soviet special operations forces cover a wide range of capabilities. The threat of the *Spetsnaz* – Soviet special operations forces – has recently attracted a great deal of attention in the West. While the red-starred equivalents of the British Special Air Service or the US Army's Rangers certainly merit this interest, they have to be seen in the Soviet context; but these forces are actually just one type of threat, part of a spectrum of Soviet forces ranging from single agents to divisions of paratroops. These forces are employed as mission requirements dictate, rather than according to a specific division of responsibilities.

Spetsnaz predecessors were used in the Russian Civil War, the Russo-Polish War, and to fight anti-Communist guerrillas in the Ukraine and Central Asia throughout the 1920s and 1930s. Soviet special warfare troops were used to create and reinforce

partisans after 1941 as well as striking directly at German rear areas. After the war, they were used extensively in the bloody but little-publicized campaigns against anti-Communist guerrillas in Poland, Ukraine and the Baltic Republics. They were instrumental in the Soviet invasion of Czechoslovakia in 1968 and of Afghanistan in 1979.

In addition to the Soviets' longer-term goal of spreading *dezinformatsiya* ('disinformation') which aims to neutralize potential enemy opposition, discredit allies, and suggest community of interest with the Soviet Union, Soviet special warfare assets can act to undermine national resistance through political measures. This is a key means of striking directly at an enemy's strategic fighting capability.

Soviet special warfare use in a future conflict would stress absolute secrecy. This might actually inhibit the use of some forces before H-Hour because inadvertent disclosure might have far-reaching consequences. The Soviets would use detailed planning and coordination between the different forces, and while they might be divided, tactically and administratively, unity of command would be reflected in their actual use.

Resupply would be either from enemy stocks or by linking up with conventional Soviet forces. Soviet special warfare forces would be employed together with other conventional long-range systems. *Spetsnaz*, air, artillery, paratroops, surface-to-surface missiles would all work on the

Left: An artist's impression of a Soviet special operations forces training facility. In addition to the traditional wood barracks, it has physical training equipment and weapons to practice the placing of demolition charges. (US Department of Defense)

same detailed target list (with alternative targets), each target to be hit by different means. Effective, secure communications are required to tie this all together.

SPETSNAZ AND SOUTHERN ASIA

The *Spetsnaz* brigade in the Transcaucasus Military District is especially important because of its potential wartime mission in southern Asia. *Spetsnaz* forces were vital during the opening days of the Soviet invasion and have played a significant role in the war in Afghanistan, especially since 1984. They have the potential to be similarly significant in any future conflict in southern Asia, such as an invasion of Iran or Pakistan.

The chance of US and Soviet ground forces meeting on the battlefield for the first time since 1920 is probably higher in southern Asia than anywhere else. The overall impact of the war in Afghanistan will not be seen until the nature of the regimes that emerge post-Zia in Pakistan and post-Khomeini in Iran are apparent. In both cases, it is unlikely that the new governments will be happy and secure.

The Soviets will probably try to manipulate any instability to ensure that any successor government is more likely to be responsive to the wishes of Moscow. This is unlikely to involve troops crossing borders, although geopolitical leverage can be exerted by strong Soviet southern theatre forces in both the Soviet Union and Afghanistan. The expansion of the airbases at Shindand and Kandahar in southern Afghanistan, far beyond the facilities required for that war, gives them a power-projection base close to the Gulf. The Transcaucasus military district *Spetsnaz* brigade would be part of that power projection capability. Thus, while, in dealing with these new governments, it is likely that the Soviets will, in preference to outright invasion, rely on normal diplomacy, internal penetration and external pressure to pursue policy goals, invasion is a possibility that cannot be dismissed. Afghanistan may have shown the Soviets that they can use force outside their borders in southern Asia without necessarily facing an insurmountable crisis.

Russia has invaded or occupied parts of Persia eleven times since the eighteenth century. In Moscow, Iran is seen as the key to the entire region. The importance of the oilfields on both sides of the Gulf and the straits of Hormuz, through which so much of the world's oil must pass, gives this long-standing interest an increasing impor-

Below: These troopers, with airborne berets, striped vests, and camouflage suits, carry AKD 5.45mm assault rifles. The troopers of the *Raydoviki* companies of the

Spetsnaz brigade would be similarly armed and equipped.

tance. The internal situation in Iran is likely to become unstable on the death of the Ayatollah.

The sub-continent also represents a policy objective dating back to Tsarist times. Warm water ports such as Karachi, or even ports on the Makran coast, could provide an outlet to the Indian Ocean.

Pakistan also is threatened with internal instability. The Soviets have already been supporting Pathans and Baluchis who have taken Moscow gold to fight the Islamabad government.

Spetsnaz are one of the most significant strengths of the Soviet military. They provide a broad spectrum of posibilities for

conflicts in southern Asia that have the potential to influence the capability of the United States to contribute to the security of either of the two regions on which Afghanistan borders: Iran and the Gulf to the west, Pakistan and the sub-continent to the east.

In Europe, the calculus of deterrence is well established and remains, in the 1980s, credible. The Soviets cannot help but be aware that any military action will risk a nuclear conflict. That is one of the reasons why the Soviet Union is not likely to use its military power on the battlefield there, for it would put at risk all of the Soviet Union. That calculus is not applicable in southern Asia, despite the announcement in 1980 by the then President, Jimmy Carter, that it will exist. The US Central Command, its combat forces based in the USA, is much less credible as a conventional deterrent or as a forward defence than US forces in Europe, in place for a generation and well integrated into an allied command structure. The Soviets have a scope for miscalculation in southern Asia that they do not have on the Central Front.

This means that there may be a need for an ability to wage war without divisions of tanks crossing borders. Soviet special operations forces could be used to help create insurgencies in Iran or Pakistan, training and acting as advisers to domestic insurgents. They are a low-profile, surgical force that would represent but one step in escalation of Soviet activity. The commitment of such forces would be certainly less

likely to produce a full-scale crisis than an Afghanistan-style invasion.

If the tanks should move, however, they will find their way greatly eased by Soviet special operations forces. As they did in Czechoslovakia in 1968 and Afghanistan in 1979, these forces would have the advantage of surprise. They would destroy or render incapable the central government and its communications systems. They would seize key airfields and chokepoints. Such capabilities are important for a potential future European conflict, but more so for one in southern Asia, where distances are greater, communications nets limited, and the Soviets would have difficulties massing overwhelming forces. In such a situation, a small force inserted by helicopter or parachute might well be able to accomplish a mission which a full division, arriving overland a week later against an alerted enemy, might find impossible. Successful use of these forces in southern Asia could have the potential to pre-empt or even preclude US intervention and deployment in the area in a way that would not be possible in Europe.

■ ORGANIZATION OF SPETSNAZ

Total *Spetsnaz* strength is reported to include 41 independent companies, 16–24 independent brigades, four naval brigades, twenty Intelligence units, three 'diversionary' regiments, and a large

Right: Soviet troopers in snow camouflage prepare a detonator.

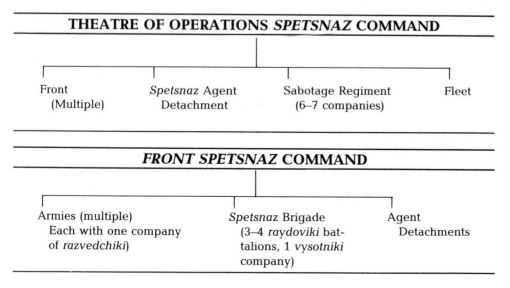

THEATRE OF OPERATIONS *SPETSNAZ* COMMAND

Front (Multiple)	*Spetsnaz* Agent Detachment	Sabotage Regiment (6–7 companies)	Fleet

***FRONT SPETSNAZ* COMMAND**

Armies (multiple) Each with one company of *razvedchiki*)	*Spetsnaz* Brigade (3–4 *raydoviki* battalions, 1 *vysotniki* company)	Agent Detachments

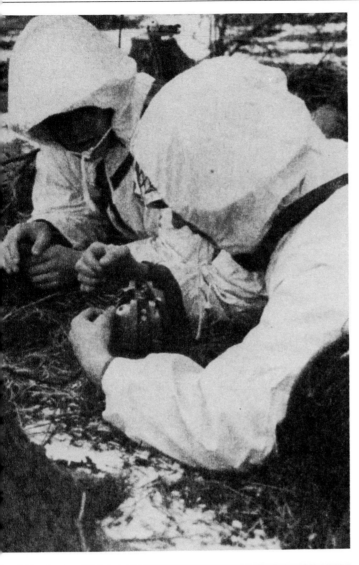

number of foreign saboteurs to be activated on *Spetsnaz* orders.

In addition, Western sources report that there is a central *Spetznaz* brigade and Intelligence centre directly under central GRU command in Moscow. The GRU is the Central Directorate of Intelligence of the Ministry of Defence, but it is more than just an analysis and reporting agency. It runs networks of agents throughout the world – especially in the West – alongside those of the KGB, the Soviet secret service. It also has its own military commando-style units.

Three of the Theatre of Operations-level TVD commands have a *Spetsnaz* regiment. Each army has long-range reconnaissance companies. Independent *Spetsnaz* companies, made up of 115 men including nine officers and ten warrant officers, would, on sabotage operations, move in groups of fifteen or more. Each company has a communications platoon with secure transmission equipment having a range of 1,000 kilometres. *Spetsnaz* brigades of 1,500 men include a headquarters company, three or four parachute battalions and supporting units.

Each fleet of the Soviet Navy has its own *Spetsnaz* brigade. It has been reported that each *Spetsnaz* naval brigade has a detachment of midget submarines (some of which were spotted in the early 1980s off Sweden and possibly off Japan and Alaska as well), two or three battalions of frogmen, one parachute battalion and supporting units.

■ SPETSNAZ TRAINING

The *Spetsnaz* brigade in the Transcaucasus Military District is probably made up of a variety of troops with differing specialities. The reason is that most of the *Spetsnaz* enlisted men are still two-year conscripts. It is more effective to train them thoroughly in one set of skills and have a wide range of special forces units, each reflecting a different operational specialty.

The brigade's troopers probably do not know they are *Spetsnaz*; they have almost certainly never heard the term. They know they are paratroopers; they know the five-digit code for their unit; they know their unit carries on the traditions and combat record of a division that fought in the Great Patriotic War; they train in scouting, demo-

TOTAL *SPETSNAZ* STRENGTH

Diversionary Regiments (7–800 men) (one per theatre of operations)	3
Spetsnaz Brigades (1,000–1,300 men) (one per Military District, Fleet, Group of Forces)	24
Long-range reconnaissance companies (115 men) (one per Army)	41
Agent detachments (20–110 men)	27+

Total strength: 29,495–37,435 men

FLEET *SPETSNAZ* COMMAND

Spetsnaz Brigade (With one anti-VIP assassination company, one midget sub battalion, two-three frogman battalions, one parachute battalion)	Agent Detachments

lition, or free-fall parachuting. The place of the *Spetsnaz* in the Soviet way of war is certainly not apparent from within the units.

All Soviet airborne and reconnaissance troops stress areas of training that are likely to be required by the *Spetsnaz*: unarmed combat, superior physical conditioning, parachute-qualification, training in heliborne operations. The bulk of *Spetsnaz*, while tough and fit troops, are unlikely, as two-year conscripts, to be all-around 'super-soldiers' on the model of the British Special Air Service or the US Special Forces. Rather, each sub-unit is trained in one specialty. This is why they have so many different types of forces.

The Soviet experience in Afghanistan suggests that airborne troopers, all of whom have complete pre-conscription military training, are also more likely to be effective in any one of many specialist roles. *Spetsnaz* or airborne troops would not be sent, untrained, to Afghanistan as some line division personnel have been in the past.

It is reported that *Spetsnaz* officers are trained at the 'reconnaissance faculty' of the Kiev Higher Arms School and the 'special faculty' of the Ryazan Higher Airborne School. Senior staff officers are trained at the 3rd Faculty of the GRU Academy.

EQUIPMENT

The *Spetsnaz* are known to be equipped with a number of special-purpose systems. In Afghanistan, they have used silenced 7.62mm AKMS assault rifles, although the silencer is an inefficient wartime-vintage design which requires the use of subsonic ammunition, and this helps reduce effective range to fifty metres or less. The silencers themselves are of an inefficient and obsolescent design. P6 silenced 9mm pistols have also been widely used, starting in 1985. Other items of equipment identified by the Afghans as used by Soviet forces carrying out 'commando' tactics include: AK-74 'Kallikov' and AKSU 'Krinkov' 5.45mm rifles, PKM 7.62mm general-purpose machine-guns, RPG-7s, RPG-18s (used against Afghan supply vehicles and as anti-sniper weapons),

Below left: A mixed formation of Warsaw Pact special forces – those in the foreground are Hungarian – are trained in unarmed combat against a bayonet.

Below centre: *Spetsnaz* training includes a broad range of unconventional combat techniques. Here a Soviet soldier throws a knife at a target while jumping over what appears to be a picket fence – certainly a memorable stunt, if of limited military utility.

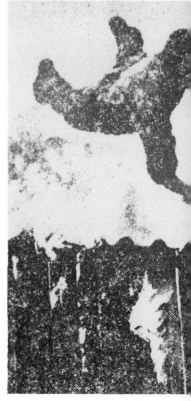

BG-15 under-barrel 40mm grenade-launchers mounted on Kalashnikovs, a larger than usual percentage of rifles with telescope sights, and AGS-17 30mm automatic grenade-launchers.

Another weapon known to be used by *Spetsnaz* in Afghanistan is a spring-loaded throwing knife with a range of fifteen metres. However, most *Spetsnaz* weaponry is standard Soviet material. They are reportedly to be equipped with R-350M man-portable tactical radios which employ secure burst transmission, man-portable radio direction-finding sets, and a wide variety of infantry weapons.

These forces are reported by the Afghans as frequently wearing body armour. Because many of the operations are apparently heliborne, it is likely that the body armour is taken aboard the Mi-8 Hip helicopters – probably, if similar to US practice, to be sat upon by the troopers.

FORCES AND MISSIONS

Spetsnaz would be vital in any future conflict in Europe. When the Soviets decided to develop the capability to fight and win a war in Europe with or without the use of nuclear weapons, they could no longer count on a nuclear strike to take out crucial targets: nuclear delivery systems and stockpiles, targeting means, headquarters, communications centres or bridges. This required the development of not only long-range conventionally armed weapons and air-power, but of special forces that could destroy them as well. *Spetsnaz*, backed up by the troops of Guards Airborne Divisions, were able to seize key objectives in Prague in 1968 and Kabul in 1979, helping to pre-empt any chance of organized resistance. They would try to do the same in Brussels, Bonn or London, linking up with KGB and GRU agents-in-place. This need to carry out a broad range of missions requires a broad range of forces.

Reconnaissance troops, designated *Razvedchiki* (scouts), are found in each Soviet division. One company of each divisional reconnaissance battalion is trained for long-range reconnaissance operations. Army-level headquarters also have a reconnaissance company that is

Below right: Soviet troopers in camouflage suits at bayonet practice. Spetsnaz have much better unarmed combat training than most Soviet soldiers.

jump-trained. Equivalent to the US Army's LRRP companies, the army-level units and possibly other independent units may be considered as *Spetsnaz*. Training probably emphasizes observation and signalling.

Raydoviki (raiders), are apparently similar to US Ranger battalions, and operate in company- and battalion-sized forces. They are apparently all jump-trained. They would also be used to train partisans behind enemy lines. *Raydoviki* seem particularly well suited to a limited war situation. The Transcaucasus Brigade would probably contain mainly this type of *Spetsnaz*; training for such a unit would be likely to emphasize light infantry tactics and demolition.

The types of *Spetsnaz* that the Soviets term *Vysotniki* are similar to US Special Forces and operate in special, mission-tailored small-sized teams for deep air-borne sabotage, reconnaissance and Intelligence penetrations behind enemy lines. They are trained in HALO (high altitude, low opening) parachute techniques. The Transcaucasus Brigade would probably have a small company of these troops, comprised mainly of officers, warrant officers, and extended service NCOs.

The Soviets have recently used the term 'mountain troops' to describe a type of unit in current service. This, together with an increased Soviet emphasis on mountain warfare tactics and techniques, probably indicates that the Soviets have deployed a specialized type of unit for effective use in mountains. These may be new units added to the Soviet order of battle. More probably, they are airborne, motorized rifle, or *Spetsnaz* units that have received special-ized training and equipment for mountain operations, which was believed to be a Soviet practice even before the war in Afghanistan.

There are also reports that Soviet forces are building two training centres in Afghanistan, one near Shindand and one near Farah, for newly created mobile desert warfare units possibly designed to strike against the Strait of Hormuz.

In addition to its Intelligence agents, the GRU (Main Military Intelligence Direc-torate) has a number of 'diversionary bat-talions'. This is a broad term and probably includes several types of specially trained units. GRU troops, both in uniform and in disguise, were apparently involved in the taking of Kabul in 1979. GRU troops are reportedly trained in a wide variety of Intelligence and commando tasks and in the use of Soviet and foreign weapons.

GRU diversionary troops report directly to the Intelligence Directorate of the General Staff. They act to support stra-tegic, operational, and tactical military and political objectives, hitting key targets – nuclear-related bases, headquarters, air-fields, communications centres – with the aid of agents-in-place and sympathizers.

GRU Diversionary Troops include teams which can operate in civilian clothes or enemy uniform. They can infiltrate objec-

Right: Afghanistan has seen the re-emergence of specialized Soviet mountain forces, capable of special operations in a wide range of terrain. (US Department of Defense)

Left: Two *Razvedchiki* scout from the top of their BRDM scout car during a long-range reconnaissance patrol.

tives before hostilities commence, and include specially trained teams to kill important individuals.

In a coordinated offensive, GRU teams would move by sea, parachute, or helicopter towards their objectives on the day before the outbreak of war. KGB teams would penetrate further in advance, usually wearing civilian clothes and concentrating at safe houses.

The KGB special purpose units are thought to have sabotage and assassination as primary missions, targeted against the civilian sector. They would cooperate with agents-in-place and sympathizers. They remain under KGB command.

Paloodra! (Look out below!) is the traditional battle
cry of the Naval Infantry making a dismounted
assault on a beach. Black berets can be worn in place
of the more usual steel helmets.

7

63RD GUARDS NAVAL INFANTRY BRIGADE, PECHENGA, KOLA PENINSULA

T HE Black Death (Der schwarze Tod) was the name given by imaginative *Wehrmacht* soldiers to their Russian opponents who wore the dark jumpers and striped T-shirts of the *Morskaya Pekhota* – the Soviet Naval Infantry. Some 600,000 Soviet sailors served ashore, participating with the Soviet Army in 114 amphibious operations, as well as many of the crucial battles of the Eastern Front.

Despite this distinguished combat record, the Naval Infantry were reduced to cadre strength, by 1948, only to be revived in about 1960 under the leadership of Admiral Sergei Gorshakov, the then Commander-in-Chief of the Soviet Navy. Gorshakov, not only remembered their wartime value, but foresaw the need for a force of sea-soldiers as the Soviet Navy started to look beyond coastal waters. The

revitalized Naval Infantry were first fully revealed in July 1964 Black Sea exercises. By 1965, the Naval Infantry was 3,000 to 4,000 strong, and a school for Naval Infantry officers had been established at Vyborg.

Since then, the force has expanded and today the Naval Infantry of the Northern, Baltic and Black Sea Fleets each consist of one active and one mobilization-only Naval Infantry Brigade and one *Spetsnaz* brigade (special forces group). The Pacific Fleet's Naval Infantry component has been considerably strengthened, and now consists of a Naval Infantry Divisional HQ, two active Naval Infantry Brigades, and one or more *Spetsnaz* brigades. Naval Infantry guard battalions provide security for naval shore installations.

Peace strength of the Naval Infantry is probably over 18,000, mobilization

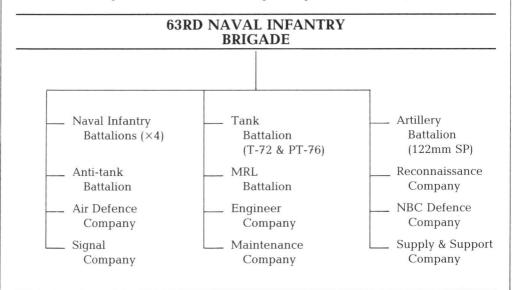

63RD NAVAL INFANTRY BRIGADE

- Naval Infantry Battalions (×4)
- Anti-tank Battalion
- Air Defence Company
- Signal Company

- Tank Battalion (T-72 & PT-76)
- MRL Battalion
- Engineer Company
- Maintenance Company

- Artillery Battalion (122mm SP)
- Reconnaissance Company
- NBC Defence Company
- Supply & Support Company

strength three times this level. The Soviet Navy has, in recent years, not only received more and better equipment in the form of hovercraft landing craft, specialized amphibious warfare ships, and even wing-in-ground effect craft, but they have also become more skilful at using their equipment. Recent exercises show Soviet amphibious capability to be mature and yet still growing.

The Soviets have made an effort to raise the Naval Infantry to an élite force. This means, in Soviet terms, allowing it a higher quota of recruits with pre-conscription military training and of higher intelligence. The Soviets have claimed that the Naval Infantry has a higher re-enlistment rate than other armed services, indicating that they do perceive themselves as an élite. Since the 1970s, increasing mention has been made in the Soviet Press of Naval Infantry troopers receiving airborne training and it is probable that the reconnaissance companies and the special forces groups are jump-qualified. Each brigade may be able to field an airborne unit of battalion size or larger equipped with BMD AFVs. Other Naval Infantry troopers receive training in mountain and arctic warfare. Each Naval Infantry Brigade is organized with a large support element to make it self-sufficient for assault operations, and can be divided into four battalion assault forces.

THE 63RD GUARDS NAVAL INFANTRY BRIGADE AND SCANDINAVIA

Probably the most significant single operational unit in the Soviet Naval Infantry is the 63rd Guards Naval Infantry Brigade of the Red Banner Northern Fleet. Significantly, it carries the honour title 'the Kierkenes Brigade' – from the town in northern Norway that was the site of the 63rd's largest amphibious battle during the Second World War. There, despite the Soviet lack of specialized amphibious warfare equipment or sophisticated planning capability, the Naval Infantry were able to overcome determined German resistance. Today, in their garrison at Pechenga, the former Finnish town of Petsamo, the 63rd

63RD NAVAL INFANTRY BRIGADE

MEN	3,000
T-72 Tanks	44
PT-76 light amphibious tanks	44
BTR-60PB or BTR-70 APCS	145
122mm SP howitzer M-1974 2S1	24
BM-21 122mm MRL	24
BRDM-2 SP ATGM launcher	12
SA-13 SP SAM launcher	4
ZSU-23-4 SP AA gun	4
SA-7 or SA-14 SAM launchers	36
RPG-16 AT weapon	120
AGS-17 30mm grenade-launcher	24
RPK-74 5.45mm LMG	120

looks not only towards the scene of past victories, but beyond.

Scandinavia has been a Russian strategic interest for centuries. Whether from the Baltic or the White Sea, the maritime routes from Russia to the outside world must go around Scandinavia. This has been evident from the time of Peter the Great's Northern War against Sweden to the grounding of a Soviet submarine armed with nuclear weapons in Swedish territorial waters in 1982.

Because these routes to the West are maritime, and because of the difficulty of land approach, the Navy must feature in any Soviet moves against Scandinavia. But for the Soviet Navy, Scandinavia has a value greater than itself. It lies between the Soviet Navy's bases and NATO's Atlantic supply lines. Scandinavia can also protect Soviet forces, especially the ballistic missile submarines, who can interpose it between their open-ocean bastions and NATO naval forces. The Soviet Northern Fleet, from its bases at Murmansk, Archangel and Polyarnoe, must use Scandinavia in accomplishing both its primary mission of protecting the ballistic missile submarines; and its secondary mission of offensive operations in the North Atlantic. The seizure of northern Norway would serve both objectives. It would deny to NATO the bases and the use of NATO's SOSUS anti-submarine tracking system, while providing the Soviets with forward bases.

The 63rd Guards Naval Infantry Brigade provides, together with the *Spetsnaz*, the

Right: Special operations are one area where the Soviet capability in a conflict in Europe would be considerably augmented by the forces of their Warsaw Pact allies. These special forces troopers of the East German Army would probably be deployed by parachute, helicopter or in suitable armoured vehicles while wearing *Bundeswehr* uniforms.

Below: BTR-60PBs of the 63rd Guards Naval Infantry Brigade on *Alligator*-class LST *029* during the 1986 amphibious warfare exercise of the Red Banner Northern Fleet. The eleven BTR-60PBs of a full company are parked as deck cargo. Each is painted on the side with the Soviet naval ensign, which is frequently applied to Naval Infantry vehicles. (Royal Norwegian Air Force)

Right: Naval Infantry hit the beach, dismounting from their BTR-60PB APCs. *Alligator*-class LSTs wait 3,000m offshore. (US Navy)

Northern Fleet's Naval Infantry strength. Much of the training of the Northern Fleet's Naval Infantry Regiment has been oriented towards spearheading an invasion of Norway. In addition to the garrison at Pechenga, only twenty kilometres east of the Norwegian border, there is also a forward base camp at Linakhamari, ten kilometres north of Pechenga.

The 63rd Guards Naval Infantry Brigade has gone to sea for several large-scale exercises since 1968. In these exercises, it has invaded desolate, rocky coasts with follow-on echelons of motorized rifle units. An amphibious invasion of Norway, possibly several hundred miles south of the Soviet border, would definitely appear to be part of the main objectives of Soviet amphibious forces.

While the 63rd Naval Infantry Brigade appears to be oriented towards operations in Norway, it and the *Spetsnaz* can have a longer reach. Naval Infantry forces – either a battalion or, more probably, special

Left: Soviet Naval Infantry belonging to one of the forces attached to some of the Soviet Navy river flotillas – such as the Danube and Amur River flotillas – board a river gunboat from their BTR-60PA. The Naval Infantry force of each flotilla is estimated to be about a battalion in strength. (US Navy)

SOVIET APCS AS USED BY NAVAL INFANTRY

Right: BTR-60s of the Soviet Naval Infantry leave an LST for the 3,000-metre, 20-minute swim to the beaches. These are open-topped BTR-60P models, which have now been passed down from the 63rd Guards Naval Infantry Brigade to its 'shadow' mobilization-only Naval Infantry brigade.

	BTR-60PB	BTR-70
Crew	3 (cdr, driver, gunner) +8 passengers	3 (cdr, driver, gunner) +8 passengers
Weight (mt)	10.2	11.0
Length (m)	7.22	7.50
Width, overall (m)	2.82	2.90
Height, overall (m)	2.31	2.30
Engine	2×6-cyl, 90hp, gasoline	2×6-cyl, 100hp, gasoline
Speed:		
Road (km/hr)	80	80
Water (km/hr)	10	10
Fuel capacity (litres)	290	290
Road range (km)	500	500
Trench crossing (m)	2.00	2.00
Vertical Step (m)	0.40	0.40
Max. gradient	30°	30°
Fording (m)	amphibious	amphibious
Armour (max.):		
Hull (mm)	9	10
Turret (mm)	7	7
NBC Protection	filtration & overpressure system	filtration & overpressure system
Introduced	1967	mid-1970s
Gun calibre	1×14.5mm	1×14.5mm
Traverse	360°	360°
Elevation	−5°–+30°	−5°–+30°
Stabilization	no	no
Fire control	telescopic sight	telescopic sight
Basic load (rd)	500	500
Secondary armament	1×7.62mm	1×7.62mm

AMPHIBIOUS ASSAULT – NAVAL INFANTRY COMPANY

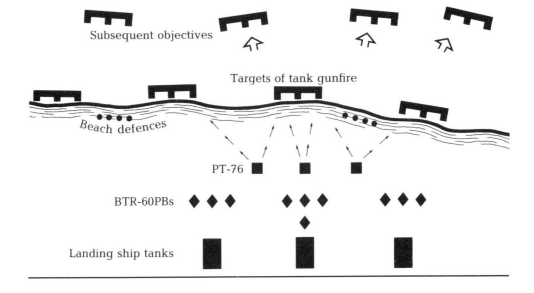

Subsequent objectives

Targets of tank gunfire

Beach defences

PT-76

BTR-60PBs

Landing ship tanks

forces troopers – coming ashore in Iceland could disrupt NATO naval forces. The continued construction and overseas deployment of the longer-ranged Soviet amphibious warfare ships and the demonstrated Soviet ability for projecting special warfare teams – from submarines, by infiltrating them in peacetime, or air-inserted – means that Iceland is not the only NATO base that could be attacked by the Naval Infantry. Bases in Norway, Greenland, the Faroes, The United Kingdom, or the Azores could be invaded. While none of these could be supplied or held, there is a

Below: Naval Infantry vehicles do not always have to swim ashore. These BTR-60PBs have been brought to the beach by *Alligator*-class LSTs. (US Navy)

potential for disrupting NATO efforts which might outweigh the loss of any forces used.

As during the Second World War, Soviet Naval Infantry operates in close cooperation with the Soviet Army. The Soviet Army will have to look to air and sea

transport to bring its forces to bear in a battle for Norway. Then, elements of a motorized infantry division could be transported on lighters aboard ship (LASH) or the roll-on roll-off (RO-RO) type of merchant ship, to reinforce a bridgehead seized by the Naval Infantry, Airborne Forces, or combined actions by both.

The Soviet Navy could certainly not secure northern Norway by itself. The Soviet Army has a corps of two motorized rifle divisions in the Kola Peninsula, along the Norwegian border. The Leningrad Military District also includes a Guards Airborne Division and an air assault brigade which could provide vertical envelopment for an invasion. Yet the Soviets are aware of the limits of combined arms mechanized forces such as motorized rifle divisions in arctic and sub-arctic terrain. Usually road-bound, they are vulnerable to ambush, flank attack, and defeat in detail. The winter war with Finland in 1939–40 taught the Soviets some costly lessons in these tactics. While the Soviets have not turned away from using motorized rifle formations in Scandinavia (they have trained the divisions in the Kola Peninsula for amphibious operations), they are not the true specialists in Soviet amphibious warfare. That distinction is reserved for the Naval Infantry.

MISSIONS AND CAPABILITIES

The Soviet Naval Infantry is still very much that: Naval Infantry. The minimal autonomy of the Naval Infantry is reflected by the fact that it has only one General Officer. Thus, the Naval Infantry is unlikely to have any great imput into the formulation of Soviet military policy.

The Naval Infantry is not comparable to the air-ground forces with world-wide mobility of the US Marine Corps, or the commando and specialized light infantry role performed by the British Royal Marines and Royal Netherlands Marines. Although it shares the amphibious mission of its NATO counterparts, which the 63rd Brigade could one day encounter on the hills of Norway, the Soviet Naval Infantry exist primarily to support the Soviet Navy in accomplishing its mission. Certainly the

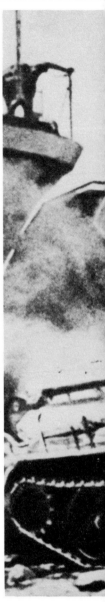

Left: Soviet troopers train on an assault course.

Above: A T-55 of the Soviet Naval Infantry comes ashore from an *Alligator*-class landing ship tank. The Naval Infantry uses both 100mm gun- and flamethrower-armed versions of the T-55 and never adopted the T-62. T-72s started to replace the T-55s in the mid-1980s. (US Navy)

securing of the Norwegian coastline could be part of that mission.

In addition to its primary mission of amphibious assault, the Naval Infantry has a number of roles that comparable Western forces do not have. They man the weapons on amphibious warfare ships. They crew the hovercraft. They function as beachmasters for the movement of Army forces and are apparently trained in field construction to assist in this mission. With significant naval mutinies taking place in the 1970s – including the crew of a destroyer of the Twice Red Banner Baltic Fleet who locked up their officers and took

off for the West (but didn't make it) – the Naval Infantry may have the mission of keeping an eye on its Naval comrades.

But amphibious assault remains the primary mission. The Naval Infantry found itself, in the 1960s, without any coherent system for amphibious operations. While some of the Second World War operations, notably the taking of Petsamo and Kierkenes along with Port Arthur and Darien in the Pacific, provided some guidance, the Soviet Naval Infantry has had to develop its own amphibious doctrine. Part of this process has been the staging of large-scale annual exercises.

In these, the Naval Infantry's basic mission of amphibious assault, in conjunction with either motorized rifle or airborne units, or alone, has been refined. These assaults are classed as either *strategic* (projecting forces to open up a new theatre of operations), *operational* (landings to support the operations of Soviet forces in a theatre of operations) or *tactical* (landings to support a specific battle).

It seems likely, at present, that Soviet Naval Infantry would probably be chiefly used in operational landings in support of wartime actions of the Soviet Navy. The small size of Naval Infantry combat units and their élite nature makes them unlikely to be committed to sustained combat alongside the Army.

As the most likely places for these operational amphibious assaults are relatively close to Soviet bases, the 63rd would probably strike at the Norwegian Coast. Similarly, the strong Naval Infantry in the Pacific is a result of the need for a stronger amphibious assault capability in the event of a war against China.

The Naval Infantry is a relatively light force and would not be optimally employed in close, intense and sustained combat which would soon lead to its 'burning out' and being rendered ineffective. Because of this, a Naval Infantry Brigade is considered the assault echelon of a Soviet Army motorized rifle division. Once the motorized rifle division is ashore, the Soviets envisage it as relieving the Naval Infantry and continuing the offensive.

Once withdrawn, the Naval Infantry unit would, if required, be sent into another invasion immediately. The Soviets point out that this was done in as little as 36 hours in their brief campaign against the

Above: The 63rd Guards Naval Infantry Brigade can use these *Aist*-class hovercraft for rapid amphibious thrusts. Each machine is capable of lifting four PT-76 light tanks, one T-72M main battle tank or 220 troops. While BTR-60s and BTR-70s are hazardous to use in high seas, hovercraft are capable of operating in a wider range of conditions. (US Navy)

Japanese in 1945, and they would probably act in a similar manner in the future.

AROUND THE WORLD WITH THE NAVAL INFANTRY

The Soviets, with the aid of their Warsaw Pact allies, have a large amphibious capability in the Baltic. In The Twice Honoured Red Banner Baltic Fleet 76th Guards Naval Infantry Regiment and the *Spetsnaz* are supplemented by substantial Polish and East German amphibious warfare troops and shipping. The main Baltic operational Naval Infantry bases appear to be Baltiisk and Tallin, while Vyborg is the main training centre and site of the Officer's School. Leningrad is the probable location for the supreme Naval Infantry Headquarters and supply depot, as well as the

headquarters for the Baltic amphibious task group. In the Baltic, the obvious targets of Warsaw Pact amphibious operations would be the Danish Islands – Bornholm was taken by a Soviet amphibious operation in 1945 – Sweden, Jutland, or even Schleswig–Holstein. Exercises held there have shown that the Soviets have the capability to use forces from Poland and East Germany in the Baltic supported by airborne troops and, if necessary, nuclear weapons, with Soviet motorized rifle divisions following up the assault. Here, as in Norway, there is always the threat that such manoeuvres could be used to cloak an actual invasion.

The Red Banner Black Sea Fleet's Naval Infantry units could be used to lead amphibious invasions of Turkish territory. The main Soviet base of the Black Sea Fleet is Sevastopol, and the fleet's Naval

Infantry brigade and associated *Spetsnaz* are probably headquartered near there. In addition to these forces, there are usually enough amphibious warfare ships in the Fifth *Eskadra* to put a battalion landing team afloat in the Mediterranean. While its primary mission would appear to be peacetime power projection, it could strike at NATO bases or at the Dardanelles.

The Red Banner Pacific Fleet's major bases are Vladivostok, Sovetskaia Gavan, and Petropavlosk. Naval Infantry Battalion Assault Forces are believed to have been deployed to Cam Ranh Bay and they may have established a permanent presence there. In addition to the need for an amphibious projection capability against China, the Naval Infantry Division would probably have a mission of spearheading an amphibious invasion of Northern Japan, to be followed up by Army motorized rifle divisions. This would also secure the Straits of La Perousse for the Soviet Navy.

The Red Banner Pacific Fleet has the strongest peacetime Naval Infantry presence: two Naval Infantry brigades and a divisional headquarters as well as at least one Naval *Spetsnaz brigada* and other special warfare forces. Like their comrades in arms in the Northern Fleet, they have a tradition of victory in amphibious operations during the Second World War which,

Left: Soviet reconnaissance troops have not only binoculars, but passive image-intensifier night vision devices.

Left: A six-man dismounted reconnaissance patrol co‑ordinates with a reconnaissance vehicle. These troopers are from the Hungarian Army, but Soviet *Razvedchiki* would be similar.

Right: A Soviet M-72 motorcycle combination armed with a 7.62mm RPK LMG moves out as part of a mechanized reconnaissance patrol of BRDM scout cars.

if small and disorganized by the standards of the Western Allies, have shown how the Soviets can build up their capabilities through improved equipment and training.

The Pacific Fleet has developed a longer reach in recent years. The frequent deployments to Cam Ranh Bay and Da Nang have included amphibious warfare ships which, even if the Naval Infantry were not on board, probably carried full loads of equipment. The countries of the Pacific rim and the Pacific basin are feeling more and more the wind from Vladivostok. But this has not altered the primary focus of the Pacific Fleet. Japan must remain its primary objective, much as Norway is for the Northern Fleet. This was seen in February, 1986, when a task force of the Pacific Fleet carried out a landing exercise in the Maritime Province, despite the presence of drift ice.

The *Spetsnaz brigada* assets are believed to include a variety of manned and unmanned midget submarines, commandos, inserted from submarines, and frogmen. Teams of specialist marksmen are used for assassination of enemy leaders, and these can be infiltrated into the target nation before hostilities begin.

In addition to the four main fleets, there are Naval Infantry units with the Caspian Sea Flotilla at Baku, the Soviet Danube Flotilla, headquartered at Izmail in Bessarabia, and the Amur River Flotilla at Blaoveshchensk and Khavarosk. Each force is unlikely to exceed a battalion in size.

POWER PROJECTION

The Soviet Navy is a powerful foreign policy tool, and the Naval Infantry, in turn, is the tool for the projection of this sea-power ashore. The effective intervention in a local crisis (after an appeal for assistance), by the US Marines in Lebanon in 1958 and the Royal Marines in Kuwait in 1961, were not overlooked by the Soviets. The expansion in the Soviet Navy's field of operations, however, has led to the Naval Infantry having a proportionately larger range. An *Alligator*-class LST appeared off Angola during the 1976 crisis, showing that the Naval Infantry could make its presence felt even at considerable dis-

tance. While some Soviet deployments of amphibious warfare ships have apparently been without troops, this included at least a company of Naval Infantry, which later landed for civic action work in Angola. In 1977, other amphibious warfare ships were off the Horn of Africa during the Ogaden War.

Since 1967, the Soviets have normally had several *Alligator* and *Polnocy* class ships in the Mediterranean, which gives the Soviet Mediterranean Squadron a

Below: Soviet Naval Infantry has been lengthening its reach since the 1970s – landing ships have appeared offshore during major crises in Africa since then – but will require more landing ships like the *Ivan Rogov*, which is capable of lifting a

Naval Infantry battalion for its amphibious capability (although it is unknown whether the troops are normally embarked). The helicopter carriers of the *Moskva* class, although normally used for anti-submarine warfare, could also be used to transport a battalion of Naval Infantry in heli-borne operations, and it has been used in this way during exercises.

Despite an impressive amount of shipping, the Soviet and Warsaw Pact amphibious lift capability is essentially short-ranged, with operational objectives rather than strategic ones. The ships, and more, importantly, the doctrine are oriented towards operations that do not require the capability the US and Royal Marines have to remain at sea for long periods and at long range. Each of the Soviet Fleets can by itself lift a motorized rifle division in addition to its Naval Infantry units. In addition, Warsaw Pact forces in the Baltic and, to a lesser extent, the Black Sea, increase this capability.

battalion. The Soviets have so far only deployed two such ships, one in the Atlantic and one in the Pacific; they have the potential to underline the Soviet Navy's power projection capability. (US Navy)

8
MEN AND ARMS

DISCIPLINE, alternating between the iron and the vagabond, hard work, terrible food are all part of the daily life of a Soviet soldier. He serves in conditions much harsher than anything the US or British soldier must face. He suffers from a wide range of disadvantages that far exceed anything seen in the West – up to 25 per cent of the troops may not speak Russian (requiring the re-introduction of a formal language training programme in units in the early 1980s), little or no leave, repetitive and boring training among them. As a consequence, some soldiers drink, go AWOL, or barter government issue, but the Soviet soldier is generally disciplined and motivated, an effective if not always efficient cog in the world's most powerful war machine.

While many Soviet units and practices reflect, to outsiders, a non-rigorous, shambling Third-World approach, the Soviet soldier receives, first, foremost and always, an intense but soldierly military discipline in which he and his society see no shame. The negative sanctions against those who fall foul of this discipline loom large in their harshness, but the rewards of the system, even if minor – a technician's qualification, 'soldier of the month', even a stripe – are none the less appreciated. This is largely because the Soviet soldier comes from a military-oriented society, and his motivation flows easily from this outlook as well as from the Soviet social attitudes, attitudes that lead the soldier to circumvent the system as well as serve it. While much may be wrong with the Soviet Army, it is this that gives the Soviets the assurance that, should the Soviet soldier be called to action in Europe, he will be there

and will fight as hard as his father did in 1941–45, even if, in Afghanistan, the negative elements of the system have been apparent.

JOINING THE ARMY

Conscription, starting at the age of 18, is widespread, excepting only those who are unfit, have hardship deferments, or are in officer training programmes in universities. There are two call-ups a year, one on about May Day, the other on about 7 November. The military commissariats in each town and district – Communist Pary organizations – function as conscription boards. Each commissairiat has a quota for conscripts to be supplied to each of the five Soviet services – Strategic Rocket Forces, Army, Air Force, Navy, and Air Defence Force – as well as the KGB and MVD troops. Each of these has a quota for a different Military District or Group of Forces. The Soviets have kept up the old Tsarist practice of trying to send recruits far away from their home districts in order to foster nationalism, reduce the chance of desertion and reduce the potential for refusal if the army has to be used against internal disturbances. The send-off for the draftees is a civic occasion with speeches by local dignitaries, and the traditionally hung-over conscripts leave in a traditionally decorated train. Usually, they will receive no home leave at all during their two-year service.

The Soviet conscript is taken to a processing centre, where he is given tests, receives uniforms and equipment, and learns basic military courtesy and drill.

Those who score well on tests and have the required educational qualifications are required to become NCOs. Except for these candidate NCOs, those bound for Afghanistan, paratroopers and some technicians, all of whom will spend three to six months in training centres or training divisions, the recruit is then sent directly to his unit, without basic training or advanced training. He has supposedly learned his soldiering before he was conscripted, for every Soviet secondary school must teach its pupils military skills. In reality, it will take at least three months' training before the Soviet soldier learns his basic job and another three months before he can be considered as combat-ready. He will spend all of his two years' service with the same unit, and he may learn very little about the rest of the Army.

MILITARY LIFE

Having arrived at his unit, even though prepared for the army by his pre-conscription training; prepared for dealing with the military bureaucracy by a life spent figuring out ways to circumvent the effects of other Soviet bureaucracies; prepared for two years in a life that he know will be arduous; the Soviet soldier can still sustain considerable shock when experiencing the army at first hand.

The quality of life varies considerably throughout the Soviet Army. Some units with poor or unconcerned officers (officers who care more about their careers than their job are found as often in the Soviet Army as in some of its potential opponents) are almost like prisons. New recruits are subjected to brutal hazing, their belongings and equipment stolen for trade on the black market. But in many units a milder system prevails. Men in their first six months of service are expected to do all the fatigues for the men doing their last six months of service. These, more senior, enlisted men, even though most are still privates (PFC rank is rare, usually only three to six per platoon) exert more real authority than brand-new sergeants just back from their six-months' training. Soviet officers exploit this unofficial chain of command as much as possible, often assigning the senior privates to jobs, know-

ing they will pick and supervise a number of more junior men. Soviet soldiers, by the last six months of their service, know how to obtain extra items for barter; they know the ways in and out of barracks after hours; they know exactly what they can get away with; and thus have the power which knowledge brings.

Soviet barracks are usually long, low wooden buildings, built with a quality of workmanship and devotion to comfort that would make the traditional US 'temporary' wooden barracks appear the height of elegance, and the more modern dormitory accommodation an almost unbelievable luxury. Conscripts – NCOs included – normally live in platoon bays. Each single bed has a foot locker, and there are platoon racks for greatcoats and equipment. Some newer barracks also have a wall locker for each soldier, but the amount of non-issue belongings that a soldier may keep is strictly limited – usually only letters from home, a book or two, and perhaps a pocket chess or dominoes set. Conscripts are forbidden to keep civilian clothing.

The barracks are usually heated, in the depths of the Russian winter, only by wood-burning, pot-bellied stoves. Heat is not the only 'luxury' that the Soviet soldier must often get used to doing without. Motorized rifle and tank troopers envy the barracks of the air defence troops whose degree of comfort can be seen at one of their installations near Archangel, in the far north of Russia, which has outdoor lavatories and no hot water. What the less fortunate units had to contend with must have been uncomfortable indeed.

Army food anywhere varies greatly from kitchen to kitchen and is never received without criticism. Yet, with all this in mind, Soviet Army food is universally abhorred for its poor quality and inadequate quantity. The diet is monotonous and almost totally devoid of fresh fruit and vegetables. Units have staple dishes which are served for dinner incessantly, the most usual being the vile sort of fried fish – or some fish-like creature – that one soldier remembered his unit ate every day except two in a year. Other units have pork as their staple – Muslim and Jewish soldiers simply have to eat it or go hungry.

Soviet soldiers have many ways of improving the food situation, the most pre-

Right: Soviet soldiers on exercises in the Far Eastern Military District are offered refreshments by local inhabitants. Soviet soldiers greatly enjoy the chance to have a break from issue food and, on exercise or simple off-base duties, will try and supplement their rations, often through barter.

Right: Aid to agriculture – these soldiers have been pressed into service to help keep a forest fire from spreading to a collective farm. The lieutenant in the foreground is obviously treating this as a military operation, for he has his issue map-case out. The more mundane but more usual task of helping gather in the harvest is less amenable to a military-style approach.

valent being the unit auxiliary farm. These are often large affairs, practically run on a commercial basis, and showing the sort of productivity Soviet agriculture reserves for private plots. A unit in a good climate, with a productive garden, can improve its food almost to human standards. Soldiers will barter for food when off duty, or will try and 'acquire' it. Each unit has a canteen where the troops can buy tea, cakes, and candy at low prices. However, the Soviet soldier still gets less food and of much worse quality than his US or British counterpart.

The Soviet conscript can by no means call his free time his own. He is often 'volunteered' for hard labour on his day off. Recreation is normally limited to organized sports – usually soccer – one day during the weekend and, if lucky, one afternoon during the week as well. Organized parties of conscripts – never alone or in pairs – may be conducted by an officer on a 'cultural' trip to a concert, war memorial, museum, or some other approved site. These trips are often used as a reward for good conduct. Such entertainment as may exist is usually created by the unit's political officer, and includes quiz competitions, skits, concerts, and other amateur efforts. Because passes are so infrequent, soldiers spend most of their off-duty time in the unit Day room, called the Lenin Room, which has books (mostly non-political), chess and domino sets, and supplies of free writing paper.

The separating of such a large proportion of the army – with the obvious exception of men stationed around larger cities – from the general population presents a splendid opportunity for indoctrination and socialization; to get the young soldiers to think of themselves as part of the greater Soviet Union rather than in terms of their family, ethnic group, or locality. It also helps in maintaining preparedness, is cheap, reduces civil-military problems, and makes best use of limited training time. The problem is that it damages morale badly, and leads the Soviet soldier to look for any means of escaping from his conditions of service. It also makes him look forward to anything that will get him away from his unit, even if it means training or working.

This includes the practice of going out to help bring in the harvest every year, as many units stationed in the USSR do. The use of soldiers for 'volunteer' labour on such civilian projects is not only a waste of training time, but is tremendously inefficient, even by the low standards of Soviet collective agriculture. Soldiers usually have neither the knowledge nor the equipment to do this job properly. They frequently end up loading apples with pitchforks or dumping grain in army trucks, which leave a trail behind them as they bounce down the dirt roads.

TRAINING

Training is the main business of the Soviet soldier. After he has finished his basic and individual training during his first six months' service, he is expected to help train the next batch of incoming conscripts. The Soviet are very concerned with training – obsessed is a better word. The Soviet soldier is first and foremost a field soldier. Units may be away from their barracks for half or more of each six-month cycle. After individual basic and skills training, the remainder of each cycle is devoted to squad, platoon, company, battalion and regimental exercises, with full divisions

Below: This lad belongs to the Construction Troops of the Soviet Army. Part of the Soviet Army's ten million mobilized strength, the Construction Troops are builders rather than fighters and built much of the Baikal-Amur rail line as well as the facilities for the 1980 Moscow Olympics.

Right: Soviet officers at a military higher educational institution. The Soviet Army places great emphasis on professional military education – a senior officer may have spent up to 40% of his career in schools. (US Army)

Right: Physical training at a Soviet military installation. While the individual Soviet soldier is a field soldier and trains extensively, he is not as fit as his British or American counterpart.

Right: Training: Soviet soldiers run an obstacle course.

Left: Soviet soldiers negotiate a tunnel with flaming rags applied as part of an obstacle course in training.

Right: Much of the Soviet soldier's training is field training. He does, however, expend less ammunition of all types than his Western counterparts, in large part because of the expense. Thus there is greater use of simulators and dry-firing and sub-calibre devices. Here, however, a soldier tosses an RKG-3M shaped-charge anti-tank grenade at a wartime T-34 tank used as a target on a 'quick kill' course.

taking the field for large-scale man-oeuvres.

In the training process, NCOs and senior privates often do not know their jobs. Thus, throughout the Soviet military, the officers do the training themselves, rather than using NCOs as in the West. The Soviets make extensive use of simulators, and have less live or sub-calibre firing than the US or British Armies. The Soviets use dedicated training weapons, often of different types or models from their combat issue, which is kept in storage. A tank unit may have only one-third to one-tenth of its tanks out of storage at any time. In high-readiness units, they may have a quite different set of tanks for training. The Soviets have nothing similar to the US Army's Opposing Forces concept that has done so much to increase realism of exercises and evaluations.

Soviet training and measures of operational effectiveness are measured by standards, quotas, and norms, and achieving these become the goals, even at the expense of what they are trying to teach or improve. The Soviet soldier knows this, and so an attitude of obeying any order, but seldom volunteering, of doing any task but of working as little as possible easily takes hold. For example, ammunition handlers are evaluated on the basis of how many trucks they can load in a period of time. The soldiers soon learn how to arrange the ammunition so that a truck appears full to the checkers when it is really only two-thirds full. They would probably never do this in wartime when lives depended on their work, but it would take a lot longer to load trucks than the Soviets think it might. Much of the impact of the war in Afghanistan on the Soviet armed forces has been the realization of how wide the gap is between peacetime training, exercises and theory – and actual warfare.

Political education is part of the Soviet soldier's training. Each company has a political officer who, although he reports directly to the Communist Party, is a fully trained officer; thus, the political officer of an artillery battery is trained as an artillery officer. The weekly political education lectures each soldier attends are received with a fair amount of scepticism when they deal with internal affairs. Lectures on foreign affairs seem to be more readily accepted – the soldiers have no first-hand knowledge of the outside world to dispel the party line. Soviet soldiers are taught, for example, that the US Army is subjected to constant harangues by capitalist commissars. The best-liked feature of political education are the films – usually inspirational wartime stuff. Political officers are by no means the despised *Politruks* of the Stalin era, hated and feared by soldiers and commanders alike; often they are highly thought of by their men, who largely appreciate their efforts as combined recreation/welfare/personnel officers.

A JUG OF WINE, A LOAF OF BREAD

Alcoholism is a problem throughout Soviet society, and the Army is no exception. The Soviet Army takes great efforts to keep drink out of the hands of conscripts. None is sold in the canteen and the low pay prevents them from buying it freely when

Left: Realistic training includes urban combat in specially constructed 'battle villages', similar to those in Western armies. Here two soldiers of the KGB Border Troops train in urban combat.

off-duty. The Soviet soldier, however, makes just as great efforts to obtain alcohol, either by trading equipment for it on the black market or by moonshining ('you strain the stuff through a loaf of bread'). Alcohol is a frequent target of surprise inspections. While Soviet officers have a reputation for hard drinking, more than occasional intoxication could imperil a career. Nevertheless, many officers end up being discharged as a result of alcoholism. The heaviest drinkers are 'lifer NCOs too dumb to become warrant officers', as they have money and access to the stuff.

Afghanistan has increased the Soviet Army's drug problem. After the invasion, to try and respect the quisling government's shaky Islamic credentials, the Soviets agreed to keep alcohol from their troops in Afghanistan. Looking for an alternative, the troops found the cheap and plentiful substances that grow in Afghanistan. It seems that rear echelon troops are the greatest abusers, having more contact with the locals and without the self-discipline of the combat troops.

Desertion and AWOL rates are high. Some Western sources estimate that 40 per cent of all Soviet enlisted men are absent without leave at some time in their service. Usually, these absences are not long or permanent. Typically they consist of sneaking off post or slipping away from detail to meet a girl, have a drink, eat a decent meal, or just talk to people not in uniform. Normally, the soldiers try to get back to their units before they are missed. A few do not. Desertion is difficult in the Soviet Union, with its internal passports and ever-present secret police and their informers.

A little palm-greasing goes a long way in the Soviet Union, and the Army is no exception. The *Autokolomka* reserve system requires that civilian firms purchase their trucks from military-specification models and keep them maintained so that, upon mobilization, they can be used immediately by the Soviet Army. Teams of Army inspectors are supposed to make sure that these trucks are fit for mobilization. If they are not, however, roubles or other goodies can often still yield an acceptable report. On mobilization day, the Soviets may find themselves quite a few trucks short of what they thought they would have.

Right: Political education is seen as one of the most important elements of the Soviet soldier's training, for army service is intended to indoctrinate soldiers to serve both the nation and the party. Here a newspaper is used for a current events discussion by an artillery battery in the field.

Getting away from barracks on exercises or on an errand provides a chance to meet people and barter for things unobtainable in the Army. Such transactions are prominent in Soviet life, although considered illegal black marketeering by the government – especially as what the Soviet soldier barters is usually government issue. The bottom halves of rubberized waterproof NBC protective suits are often traded to fishermen in return for fresh fish. Issue blankets, gasoline, and other items are often exchanged for food or, the ultimate prize – a bottle of vodka. Few soldiers would try and match the tank crew in Czechoslovakia in 1986 which traded its tank for a crate of vodka. The tank was long since cut up for scrap by the time the crew came-to in the hands of the unamused authorities. The Soviet soldier will normally not, however, barter weapons or ammunition. That is a political crime, not a 'criminal' one, and carries a potential death penalty. In Afghanistan, however, Muslin soldiers sympathizing with the Resistance, and drug addicts in need, will frequently take risks and will hand over weapons and ammunition.

The miserable conditions of service, the monotonous diet, the isolation of the Soviet soldiers produces another problem – suicide. The suicide rate in the Soviet Union has always been high, although accurate figures are impossible to ascertain – officially, no one should be unhappy in a socialist state. The armed forces suffer about twice the suicide rate of Soviet society as a whole. It is viewed as a considerable problem by Soviet authorities. Suicide seems especially prevalent among the enlisted men of the Strategic Rocket Forces, the cream of the Soviet enlisted personnel. These educated soldiers spend most of their tour in small detachments at isolated missile sites in the Asian USSR. Any force that produces such a suicide rate would inevitably have questionable morale.

The punishment for any of these escapes from military discipline can be swift and certain. A dishonourable discharge stamped on his internal passport will blight the life of any Soviet citizen to a degree that Westerners can hardly imagine. The labour camps of the GULAG await black marketeers and bribe-takers. The Soviets still shoot people, even in peacetime – a number of executions were reported by reliable sources in the wake of the Soviet invasion of Czechoslovakia in 1968, and Lieutenant Belenko (the defecting *Foxbat* pilot) knew an Air Force NCO who was shot for desertion. One reason that the Soviets can get away with their terrible conditions of service is that the iron hand of repression prevents anyone from doing anything about it.

WOMEN IN THE ARMY

The Soviet Union has long boasted of the equality of women in its society. During the Second World War, women took their place in combat – most notably in the Air Force. But today, despite propaganda, the Soviet Army is as male chauvinist an organization as can be found anywhere. The number of female soldiers is very small and they are limited to traditional nursing or clerical positions. They are normally quartered in a separate compound, distant from other barracks. The Soviets consider the use of women in non-traditional military specialities purely a wartime expedient. Soviet officers have privately expressed the view that the widespread US Army use of women is destructive of effectiveness and cohesion and shows the continuing bankruptcy of the US Army.

RE-ENLISTMENT

As the Soviet soldier approaches the end of his two years, he is subjected to a considerable stream of propaganda to get him to stay with the military. Those with sufficient educational qualifications and unquestioned political loyalty can put in for officer training, which requires passing several written and oral examinations. The Soviets obtain a large percentage of their officers in this way, especially in service support units. Those not qualified for or not wanting a commission can become warrant officers, which also requires educational qualifications and examinations. Those who qualify are given a one-year training course. Warrant officers are the nearest thing the Soviet Army has to veteran British-style NCOs – wise old soldiers, able

Right: Loading a field bakery truck. Soviet rations, while improved from those that led to near-starvation in the 1968 invasion of Czechoslavakia, still depend heavily on bread.

to use any weapon or to do any job, even though most Soviet warrant officers are under the age of 30. Warrant officers enjoy the same benefits as commissioned oficers – quality uniforms instead of lumpy, ill-fitting clothes, shoes instead of boots, and access to officers' special shops which have goods unobtainable in most places in the USSR (although the really good stores are reserved for major and above).

Only a very few soldiers – never more than one to two per cent – re-enlist as enlisted men. Anyone who does becomes a sergeant automatically. Because of this low re-enlistment rate, only 5 per cent of the Soviet Army's enlisted personnel are not conscripts doing their two years. Most of the men who become sergeants do so because they are not qualified to become warrant officers. These extended service sergeants generally have a poor reputation, quite the opposite of the warrant officers. They are singled out as the worse drinkers and are often prejudiced or brutal. Their children are the single worst group of juvenile delinquents in the Soviet Union. If one of these people secures a supply sergeant position, it can mean a fortune on the black market. While their numbers contain many good soldiers, the depredations of many of these extended service sergeants can be formidable.

■ FIGHTING MEN

The Soviet soldier is paid little, fed rubbish, worked hard, and, although the average Soviet soldier is usually not ill-educated, is treated as an idiot, or a potential deserter. It is a hard and often self-defeating system, critically cutting into the supply of long-service men who are the backbone of any army. The result of all this is strangely not large-scale discontent, but a sense of pride. Despite being treated like this, Soviet soldiers, even those who have left the Army and the Soviet Union and have no love at all for Communism, retain a deep pride in having been a Soviet soldier. Since childhood, Soviet citizens are taught that service to the state is something to be proud of, not a source of shame for those who serve. The low pay – few men are able to save while doing their time – does not hurt too sorely, for the product-poor Soviet citizen does not view money as the report card of life. The Soviet soldier knows he is a valued member of society, not an embarrassment to the 'best people'. He probably knows the system is stupid. He probably would never re-enlist regardless of incentives. He does as little work as possible in peacetime; but, on the bottom line, he is a soldier, and there should be no doubt that he is prepared to fight for his homeland.

Below: A special forces team emerges from a culvert.

9

HOW THE SOVIET ARMY INTENDS TO WIN THE NEXT WAR

THE Soviet Army, like its government, really and truly does not want to fight, especially against NATO. The rise of nuclear weapons, even in an era of strategic parity or Soviet superiority, makes it unlikely that the Soviets will want to add western Europe to their empire by force of arms unless circumstances change. Rather, the strength of the Soviet Army is seen as a key element in what the Soviets term the 'correlation of forces', the Soviet power which they hope will lead, over the years, to the neutralization of Europe. Once neutralized, the Soviet Union, as the only European superpower, will hold sway, without the need for armies of occupation as in Poland or Czechoslovakia. The Soviets would like to win the next war without fighting it.

This does not mean they are not prepared to fight. Ever since its inception, the Soviet Art of War has been trying to come to grips with changing technology and the changing tactical and operational concepts of potential enemies of the Soviet Union. Even with the military having first claim on the resources of the Soviet Union, these resources are not infinite, so it must be done in an economically feasible way. To counter new conventional weapons technology, the Soviets are unlikely to break dramatically with what they have spent a great deal of money and effort to achieve – the capability to win a war in Europe without having to use nuclear weapons. They started working towards this goal in about 1967 and apparently believed they had reached it in 1982, an event marked by Brezhnev's 'no first use' statement, in which the Soviets stated that they would not be the first to use nuclear weapons in a

future conflict. Whether this reflects actual as opposed to stated Soviet government policy is less significant than the fact that it shows that the Soviet military thinks that it can win without the use of nuclear weapons.

This means that Soviet operations and tactics have a thorough imperative in the initial stage of a conventional war: the nuclear threat must be defeated. The Soviet investment in improved conventional weapons has, in large part, been intended to give them the capability of destroying enemy tactical and theatre-level nuclear weapons systems (i.e., those in Europe) during the initial, conventional period of a conflict. The means for doing this are airstrikes with conventional munitions, chemical weapons, special forces, airborne forces, helicopters, and mechanized units penetrating deep into NATO defences.

The continuing emphasis on the theme, dominating Soviet military thought since the Civil War, that the key to victory in a conventional conflict is to strike deep at the heart of the enemy defence, has become more important under the demands of this new capability. This capability also gives the Soviets the forces to strike deep at other NATO targets. The headquarters, command, control, and communications facilities, airfields, bridges, and reserve units are the framework which make possible not only the US Army's AirLand Battle operational concept, but the overall strategy of AFCENT (Allied Forces Central Europe). The Soviets would insert Operational Manoeuvre Groups, up to a division in size, through any gap in NATO defences, to penetrate 30 to 100 kilometres.

These are intended to seize key objectives and hold them until relieved. Smaller units would do the same for tactical objectives at 30 kilometres or less distance of penetration.

The Soviets fielded a new generation of heavy artillery in the 1970s. These are intended to give a long reach to artillery support of such penetrating forces. The increase in size and capabilities of Soviet helicopter forces means that not only can forces, such as the specialized air assault brigades, be inserted directly into an enemy's operational depths, but also provide close air support in the enemy rear.

One of the most significant developments has been in the realm of conventional, bomblet warheads for surface-to-surface missiles. These give the Soviets an ability to knock out airfields without having to use nuclear warheads, although the provision of chemical payloads for all these missiles shows another way the Soviets may try and 'strike deep' with non-nuclear systems.

Whether a war uses nuclear or the new, more lethal, high-technology conventional weapons in its opening stages, the Soviets would lay great emphasis on surprise. They are aware that modern conventional weaponry, if deployed and properly used, can inflict unacceptable casualties on a much larger force. The Valley of Tears Battle on 7 October 1973, where the Israeli 7th Armoured Brigade defeated a Soviet-equipped Syrian force which outnumbered it by more than six to one certainly helped to remind the Soviets that numbers alone is not the answer. They realize that, regardless of how effective a weapon system may be, it is not going to be useful if it is hit by a pre-emptive strike while still in a vehicle park. They know that surprise must be achieved if their objectives are to be attained within a few days, before the West can initiate nuclear warfare. They know that surprise will have to be 'political'. It may be impossible to hide the mobilization of troops or the movement of ships from modern reconnaissance means, but it may be possible to achieve 'political' surprise, striking in such a way and at a time when those leaders in the West who would order NATO to its battle positions along the Inner German Border would not have the time or the will to do so.

The Soviets realize that chemical weapons are potentially powerful. They have been developing new chemical weapons for years, while the West has not only not been developing new weapons, but its existing stockpiles have been allowed to deteriorate. By making extensive use of new and deadly chemical weapons, the Soviets could not only disrupt NATO forces, especially those in the rear area, but also create panic among civilian populations.

Soviet operations and tactics would emphasize continuous combat. They would fight by day and night, to keep up a degree of pressure which NATO forces would find hard to counter.

The Soviets would also continue to use electronic warfare, severely limiting NATO's use of the electromagnetic spectrum by deception, jamming or use of radio direction-finding equipment to target anyone using a radar or radio. This would be one of the main counters to the 'look deep – strike deep' approach of the US Army.

In a future war, the Soviets would try to maintain the speed and shock in their operations and tactics which they believe leads to victory. If they were able to present to NATO a situation that worsened faster than NATO could deal with it, either on the battlefield or in the minds of its leadership, it might be possible for them to achieve their goal – five days to the Rhine. In that case, the ability to strike deep or carry the war to the enemy's rear might not matter to either side.

To do this, the Soviets have well thought out systems of command and control. While Soviet low-level tactics are often stereotyped and based on battle drills, their operational-level thinking is not so limited. Soviet operational-level commanders are not limited to textbook concepts of echeloning and deployment, but rather are encouraged to carry out their assigned missions in a flexible and aggressive manner. The Soviet command, control and communications system is intended to promote this approach, as is the increasing automation of staff procedures through the use of battlefield computers.

The Soviet Army will still be two armies, if not more. There will be the high-readiness army, in East Germany, the Western

Above: After an air assault – here apparently carried out by paratroopers – the Hip-Es move off while the skirmish lines form out and leave the landing zone under simulated fire. The blank-firing attachment on the Kalashnikovs suggest that this is part of an exercise. In an actual battle, Hinds, supplemented by Hips, would be providing supporting firepower to the air assault. (US Army)

Military Districts of the USSR, in action in Afghanistan, and wherever élite forces such as the airborne or the *Spetsnaz* are stationed. This is the force the West is most concerned about, and deservedly so, for it includes weapons comparable with those used by the West, and its soldiers, though two-year conscripts, are at least as thoroughly trained as the system permits. This first force, however, is only part of the Soviet Army. The bulk of the Army is likely to remain, in the future as now, of low and moderate readiness formations in the Soviet Union, formations which rely on reservists to bring them up to strength for combat. These divisions do not practise call-ups, let alone exercise as divisions. They do not have the same high-technology hardware of the high-readiness divisions. Rather, they have older, or simpler equipment suited to the lesser skills of their reservist personnel who lack refresher training. This bifurcation is the only way the Soviets can maintain such a large army without even further bankrupting their economy.

The Soviets would see any future war in Europe as starting with an initial phase of conventional operations. All the key factors in their operational thought would be concentrated on attaining victory before the war could escalate to a nuclear exchange. They do not want to occupy a nuclear wasteland, let alone become one. The Soviet plan must be to shatter NATO in the first few days of a war. That is why surprise is so important. The Soviets will go for the weak spots in NATO's defence, remembering the old German adage that 'the best tank country is that without anti-tank defences'. They would expect to reach the Rhine in five days, the Channel in another three to five. If they could achieve the surprise they seek, they could probably succeed.

The Soviet Army has always had a numerical superiority over its enemies. They show no sign of being willing to give that up. But they have been making great investments in an attempt to match that with qualitative capabilities until now only hoped for in Moscow. The Soviets have continued to improve their ability to wage war, and the second half of the 1980s will doubtlessly include additional counters to increased NATO efforts.

INDEX